IN GOD WE TRUST
BUT ONLY AS A LAST RESORT

IN GOD WE TRUST

but only as a last resort

DANIEL OWENS

CROSSWAY BOOKS • WHEATON, ILLINOIS
A DIVISION OF GOOD NEWS PUBLISHERS

This book is dedicated to:

Pastor Harold Carlson
Retired, but still running the race

Who opened my spiritual eyes to the love and greatness of God; the abiding friendship of Jesus Christ; the reality of the Holy Spirit. Who taught me how to worship; how to love; how to trust. Who discovered my gifts; inspired me to use them; pointed me in the right direction. Who has been the most influential Christian in the lives of my wife and me over the past twenty years. We love you, and to quote a phrase that you have encouraged thousands of people with through the years. "We are for you and Janie!"

In God We Trust, but Only as a Last Resort

Published by Crossway Books
A division of Good News Publishers
1300 Crescent Street
Wheaton, Illinois

Cover design: David LaPlaca

First printing, 2000

Printed in the United States of America

Library of Congress Cataloging-in-Publication Data

Owens, Daniel 1956-
In God we trust : but only as a last resort / Daniel Owens.
p. cm.
ISBN 1-58134-213-6 (pbk. : alk. paper)
1. Trust in God. I. Title.
BV4637.O94 2000
248.4—dc21 00-009362
CIP

15 14 13 12 11 10 09 08 07 06 05 04 03 02 01 00
15 14 13 12 11 10 9 8 7 6 5 4 3 2 1

CONTENTS

Chapter 1

TO BE A CHILD AGAIN

The bumper sticker on the car in front of me said "Trust Jesus." My first thought was, *I already have*.

I clearly remember the morning I walked forward in a church service and turned my life over to Christ. As a seventeen-year-old senior in high school, I trusted the Lord Jesus Christ with my eternal soul, and I found great peace in that monumental decision. No longer would the little brass-plated prayer my mother hung on my bedroom wall haunt me. Although the prayer was simple, it held enormous ramifications to a little boy. It read:

Now I lay me down to sleep.
I pray the Lord my soul to keep.
If I should die before I wake,
I pray the Lord my soul to take.

That third line was what caused me grief each night as I went to bed. "If I should die before I wake." When I learned that God loved me, that He had provided a perfect sacrifice for my sin through His Son, Jesus Christ, and that I could know I would live with Him in heaven forever, I felt great relief. I put my trust in Jesus—and have since forgiven my mom for putting that prayer in my room!

I thought about that bumper sticker again. "Trust Jesus." At seventeen it was easy enough, or at least that's how I remember it to be. What about at forty? Do I find it as easy to trust Jesus the way I did as a teenager?

Maybe you have asked yourself that very question. Perhaps, like me, you have struggled with being able to turn the stresses of this complicated adult life over to the Lord and find peace in Him. Trusting God should be the easiest aspect of Christian living. Yet we sometimes, perhaps often, seem to have a hard time with it.

It has been said that there are three stages in a man's life. The first stage is he believes in Santa Claus. The second stage is he doesn't believe in Santa Claus. The third stage is he is Santa Claus!

I have thought many times about how nice it would be to return to that first stage in life when I believed in Santa. What I mean is, how wonderful it would be to go back to being a believing, trusting child. Then I could retreat to my own little world, a place with no stress and minimum responsibility. No worrying about raising godly kids in a very ungodly world. No feeling the pressure of paying bills. No fretting about saving for retirement. Giving no thought to keeping the cars running. I would care little about the future of my job or the cares and concerns of the church. I could just be a little boy and enjoy a life of innocence and make-believe like I once did. Do you ever feel that way?

It seems easier to trust Jesus with our eternal souls than with how we're going to make next month's house payment. It's easier to trust Jesus to forgive us for our sin than to trust Him with our relationships. It's easier to trust Jesus for the filling of the Spirit than to trust Him with the stresses and headaches of our lives.

My lack of trust doesn't mean I believe God is unwilling to help us in our time of need. It just means that my perspective of who God is and what He is capable of doing has been severely clouded. Not trusting God with the details of my life is much more of an indictment of me than of the ability of God to rule well. Despite what I know to be true, I wrestle with trusting God, as do many people across America and around the world.

But God doesn't want us to struggle. Not only does our heavenly Father encourage us to put our confidence and hope in Him, but He also commands us to do so. We can trust in God when we are faced with a crisis, such as a death in the family or personal financial collapse or a failing marriage. During those times we can take great comfort in passages such as Psalm 94:19: "When anxiety was great within me, your consolation brought joy to my soul."

Even more thrilling to me is knowing that God deeply desires that we become like children once again and put our trust in Him for our daily experiences. The author of Hebrews summed up God's heart for His children when he wrote, "Without faith it is impossible to please God."

The God of this universe is calling us. He is urging us, pleading with us, to put our trust in Him. What an invitation! And when we respond and lean on Him, that pleases Him. I cannot get over the fact that when, in childlike faith, I completely trust God for something very specific in my life, I actually bring joy to Him. I cause God to be happy.

I have three boys—two teenagers and a toddler that God recently surprised my wife and me with. I enjoy and find great delight in my sons when they put their trust in me.

What father doesn't like to hear the words, "My dad can fix anything"? Actually, I don't like those words because my wife usually fixes everything. "Tim the Toolman Taylor" I am not.

But what about, "My dad will play ball with us"? Those special words I loved to hear because I enjoyed taking my sons to the park to hit baseballs or throw around a football. My boys knew they could trust me to take them to do their favorite activities. Nothing beats the joy of watching your child and his friend walk up to you and confidently ask you to take them to the park—especially since that gives you the chance to show them that special curveball of yours.

My sons trust me, and from that trust I receive much joy and contentment. Their actions demonstrate that they trust my love for them, knowing for certain that I want to spend time with them. That also shows they trust my ability to protect them, knowing I would not allow any harm to come to them. And it proves that they trust my desire to provide for them, knowing I am the one who always buys the equipment we take to the park.

So what does my lack of trust say about my relationship to God? I am afraid it speaks volumes, and the things it says are not complimentary. How offensive and hurtful it is to my heavenly Father to see my skepticism, doubt, and sometimes even fear regarding His ability to care for me. As a father I know I would be hurt if my sons insinuated that I couldn't provide for them or protect them from harm, humanly speaking. Yet day after day you and I tell God by our actions that we don't trust Him, even though He has proved Himself to us over and over again.

We all doubt God at times. In fact, David wrote Psalm after Psalm telling God that his circumstances seemed to prove God wasn't trustworthy after all. But David always came back to what he knew and had seen firsthand as being true. Consider Psalm 22:4-5, which he wrote as a reminder of God's faithfulness:

> *In you our fathers put their trust;*
> *they trusted and you delivered them.*
> *They cried to you and were saved;*
> *in you they trusted and were not disappointed.*

In reminding himself of what God had done in the past, David was following God's command to the Jews to pass on from one generation to the next the harsh yet wonderful experiences that took place in the life and times of Israel. In fact, that's what the celebration of Passover was all about. During those eight days of personal worship, reflection, and sacrifice, the Israelites would take time to retell God's mighty works.

As the family gathered around, the elders would share at least three ways God had been and still was faithful to Israel.

First, someone would retell the story of the Exodus, the deliverance from bondage and slavery in Egypt. If he was honest, he would also tell how they got into such a mess in the first place. Who can deny that the Israelites had a way about them, a dark side that led them to follow other gods?

Second, the story of the Ten Commandments was told. I can imagine the little ones leaning forward, eyes focused on the storyteller as he shared how Moses climbed the mountain to meet God, who he had first experienced in the form of a burning bush that was not consumed! It was time for more milk and cookies because the kids really got into this story.

Third, someone would tell of the wonderful Promised Land. I am sure everyone heard how the spies sneaked in and saw the giants and were shaking in their boots, and how the Lord God later went before them in many battles. I imagine the kids were as excited as mine would be watching a good action movie on TV.

When the stories came to the end, the family spent time praising God for all He had done. That was the reason for Passover—remembering who God is and what He has done.

In the book of Deuteronomy we see Moses reciting a song to the entire assembly of Israel. The song, encompassing forty-three verses, delivers in detail the acts of God and the failures of Israel. The man of God begins by praising the greatness of God in 32:3-5:

I will proclaim the name of the Lord.
Oh, praise the greatness of our God!
He is the Rock, his works are perfect,
and all his ways are just.
A faithful God who does no wrong,
upright and just is he.

Moses then tells of the rebellion that had crept into the hearts of the Israelites, an attitude that caused the Lord's anger to burn against them, and paints a verbal picture of the good life they no longer enjoy because of their rebellion and disobedience. Moses used this song to encourage the Israelites before his death, as well as to convey a stern warning not to anger the Lord once again by their idolatry.

Throughout the Old Testament we find many of the writers reciting the history of Israel to the people. The reason for the history lesson? To cause the people to ask themselves, "Do I trust God?"

In Deuteronomy 9:23-24 Moses reflects on the actions of Israel when he says, "You did not trust him or obey him. You have been rebellious against the LORD ever since I have known you."

Moses gets right to the point. He goes straight to the heart of the matter regarding Israel's activities. They didn't trust God. They didn't trust God. They didn't trust God!

The Israelites had put their hope in something or someone else. By their actions, they cried out that they believed some other god could do a much better job of taking care of them. Another god could love them more and was more interested in their welfare. A foreign god could do more miraculous deeds than the God of heaven could. Another deity could answer their prayers more quickly. Or so they thought.

Moses said the gods in whom the children of Israel were trusting were "gods they had not known, gods that recently appeared, gods your fathers did not fear" (Deuteronomy 32:17).

God's heart was broken by the idolatry of Israel, and His anger was ignited against them.

As we look back on the Old Testament Scriptures, we shake our heads and wonder how Israel could have been so foolish as to put their trust in idols. To think that some lifeless form of wood or metal would have any power to save, heal, or direct!

> *"Of what value is an idol, since a man has carved it?*
> *Or an image that teaches lies?*
> *For he who makes it trusts in his own creation;*
> *he makes idols that cannot speak.*
> *Woe to him who says to wood, 'Come to life!'*
> *Or to lifeless stone, 'Wake up!'*
> *Can it give guidance?*
> *It is covered with gold and silver;*
> *there is no breath in it.*
> *But the* LORD *is in his holy temple;*
> *let all the earth be silent before him."*
>
> HABAKKUK 2:18-20

According to Habakkuk, the people worshiped things that had a maker and were absent of breath. In other words, the gods had no life in themselves, even though people claimed they gave life, or at least affected life. God was angry at the Israelites because they put their trust in things that were dead. They looked for the meaning of life in images made out of silver or gold. Through their sacrifices, they asked for forgiveness from carvings formed by human hands. God the Creator was not given His rightful place in their lives, teaching, or worship.

I'm sure we all agree with Habakkuk's assessment, and many of us might wonder at the naiveté that would cause someone to think otherwise.

But let me pose a question. Do you trust God? Really? Or do you have idols in your life, lifeless things like the ones Habakkuk spoke of but with a modern appearance?

A couple of years ago I was invited to speak at a conference in Nepal. I had traveled to India and other Asian countries, so I knew what to expect as far as the climate, the culture, the food, and the people. And, as always, I was excited at the opportunity to meet brothers and sisters in Christ in another country. But while there, I learned a lesson I will never forget.

One afternoon, after finishing my speaking engagements for the day, my Nepalese host and I went sightseeing, a pleasure I rarely get to enjoy. As we traveled through the picturesque (although quite congested and smoggy) streets of Katmandu, I enjoyed watching the children playing in the streets, vendors selling those famous curved knives (my son begged me to bring one home), and people cooking on open fires next to the streets. I even sampled a bit of the food. Finally we neared the most famous Hindu temple in all of Nepal.

The closer we got to the temple, the slower we had to drive to avoid hitting the vendors nearly filling the street. Several hundred yards from the temple, we decided we should get out of the vehicle and walk. In moments a flock of kids—the human variety—came up to me to sell me beads, trinkets, and miniature idols. The girls told me how much my wife would enjoy these beads and how wonderful they would look on her.

As we rounded a corner, I caught my first glimpse of the temple. It looked like something right out of an Indiana Jones movie! The temple sat just across a little river, nestled in thick trees and vines crawling with monkeys. The gloominess of the day added to the darkness of the temple.

As we walked to the edge of the river, we came upon the temple's main entrance and courtyard. The huge edifice had stairs coming down to the water's edge. To the right of me I noticed some people bathing in the river, as do many around the world who have no indoor plumbing. The river was only about fifteen feet across and was quite stagnant, but it was the only water available to these extremely poor people.

My attention was drawn back to the courtyard and the crowd of people gathered there. My host informed me that we were watching a Hindu funeral service and that they were preparing the body for cremation. I could see the dead body lying on top of layers of dried branches, like an altar. I listened as my host walked me through each step of the ceremony as it happened. I listened with a heavy heart to the family's cries and wondered what words of comfort the speaker was giving, if any.

My host told me the speaker was the high priest praying for the dead relative in hopes of bringing him back to life, reincarnated as a creature. The gods and the kind of life he lived determined which creature the man would come back as. The priest was there to assist the dead man and, of course, receive money for his prayers. The deceased had to have been a wealthy man to have this type of funeral.

As I watched them light the fire and saw the body go up in flames and heard the cries of the family grow louder, I could not help but feel a deep sense of sadness. Billions of people, not millions, but *billions* in Asia follow hundreds of millions of gods in hopes that they will have a better life the next time around.

My heart ached when I thought of the utter despair they must feel, not having the hope of heaven as we do. I agonized at the realization that they have no idea that they have a loving heavenly Father who has provided the way of salvation for them through His Son, Jesus Christ. They don't understand that sacrifices to their gods are obsolete because of the work of Christ on the cross. They live pointless lives, and then they die without a Savior.

The pain and sorrow were so deep, I had to verbalize what I was feeling. Quietly I said to my host, "I cannot understand how these people believe these idols and prayers and sacrifices are going to save them. Idol worship is so sad."

My host's response surprised me. "I have been to the West, and you, too, worship idols. It is just that your idols look different than ours here. Our idols take on the form of a monkey god or an elephant god, but your idols take on the shape of a car or a house or money or success. Your country practices idolatry as well."

With those words I was left speechless and defenseless.

Do I practice idolatry? Does America practice idolatry? Does the church here practice idolatry?

Based on the analysis my Nepalese friend gave and on the Scriptures in Habakkuk, I would have to say yes to all of the above. Although I am a follower of Jesus Christ, I began to realize that in certain areas of my life I too was worshiping idols, and that my idolatry was hindering me from growing in faith.

Not surprisingly, researcher George Barna discovered that many of the world's practices are also practiced in the church. You can take any area of ethics, morality, or godless lifestyle and find it in the church. Our youth struggle with drugs, sex, and self-esteem. Our men struggle with pornography, materialism, and self-love. Our women struggle with a sense of belonging, overreliance on physical appearance, and selfish ambition. This is the short list, but we can easily see that the church often matches the world sin for sin, idol for idol.

You and I must ask ourselves, "What difference does Jesus Christ make in our lives?" If someone were to examine my life, would they notice anything that would set me apart from my neighbors across the street?

What about you? How different are you from the people you work with?

Let's be honest here. Our lives, for the most part, are not built on childlike faith in our heavenly Father. We replace our Creator with things we have created.

If we have a financial emergency, how many of us commit that need to the Lord and ask Him to do the miraculous and provide for us? We would rather remove our half maxed-out Visa from our wallet, plop it down, and thank God for this wonderful thing called credit. Who needs God when you have a

$4,000 credit limit and five or more credit cards? Why trust God when you can trust American Express?

Trusting God with our finances is only one example. How many of us have learned to experience God and prove His faithfulness in our daily lives? How often do we go to Him in prayer with our real needs?

Sadly, we often behave like the children of Israel. What's so bad about that? First, we are saying we don't need God to fill our lives because we have filled it with other things, other idols. We have cars, houses, success, relationships, hobbies, work, sports, clothes, and countless other things that we have created to fill our lives.

Second, we are saying we have put our trust in something other then God. I know how I would feel if my sons told me they trusted someone more than me to take care of our family. How do you think God feels? And, yes, He does feel pain when you and I say by our actions that we trust the American way, the American dream, or the Bank of America to be our provider. Our materialism is destroying our trust in God.

In His Sermon on the Mount, Jesus explained quite clearly what our understanding and attitude toward our heavenly Father should be:

> *"Therefore I tell you, do not worry about your life, what you will eat or drink; or about your body, what you will wear. Is not life more important than food, and the body more important than clothes? Look at the birds of the air; they do not sow or reap or store away in barns, and yet your heavenly Father feeds them. Are you not much more valuable than they? Who of you by worrying can add a single hour to his life?*
>
> *"And why do you worry about clothes? See how the lilies of the field grow. They do not labor or spin. Yet I tell you that not even Solomon in all his splendor was dressed like one of these. If that is how God clothes the grass of*

the field, which is here today and tomorrow is thrown into the fire, will he not much more clothe you, O you of little faith? So do not worry, saying 'What shall we eat?' or 'What shall we drink?' or 'What shall we wear?' For the pagans run after all these things, and your heavenly Father knows that you need them. But seek first his kingdom and his righteousness, and all these things will be given to you as well. Therefore do not worry about tomorrow, for tomorrow will worry about itself. Each day has enough trouble of its own."

MATTHEW 6:25-34

We have read this passage and heard it quoted so many times that we can almost recite it word for word. But how many of us really believe Jesus' words and practice them? God, our Father, wants us to trust Him for our welfare, for our protection, for our children, for our food, for our very lives. It is a reasonable request, is it not? He who has made us and everything else in this world, He who loves us more than we can ever imagine or put into words, asks us to put our trust in Him.

We have turned our greatest privilege into a cliché. It is so easy to say that we trust God, but our constant worry and manipulation of situations prove otherwise. Our American currency has imprinted on it the words "In God We Trust," but those words have become a shadow of what once was. I would say the truth has become more "In God We Trust, but Only as a Last Resort."

Three years ago I was invited to speak at an evangelistic campaign in Lahore, Pakistan. Normally I would jump at the chance to go anywhere to speak, but this invitation caused me a bit of agitation.

Think about it. An American Christian evangelist going into Muslim Pakistan to speak about Jesus Christ in an outdoor stadium named after Muammar Gadhafi. Add to that the anxiety of leaving my wife and two teenage sons with a newborn baby.

I began to play out in my mind what would happen if I were killed. I began to worry about the potential of being kidnapped as other missionaries had, and my family not hearing from me for years, if ever.

So I phoned Brother Andrew of Open Doors and sought his counsel on whether or not I should go. He advised me that this campaign was an invaluable opportunity—not for me, but for the Gospel.

I wrote back to the leadership in Pakistan, telling them I gladly accepted their invitation. To be honest I really was not that glad.

As my time of departure for that campaign drew near, I was distracted by Taylor's recent birth. Being forty and having two teenagers and a new baby boy in the house was quite an adjustment. But then to depart for Pakistan . . .

One evening just before I left my dad called me. I could tell he was troubled, and he proceeded to tell me why. "Dan, why do you have to go to Pakistan?" he asked. "You have a five-week-old baby, you've already preached all around the world, and the State Department has advised you not to go. Why do you have to go?"

It had been a long time since my dad had chewed me out, but I knew he was doing it out of love for my family and me. And his questions were the same ones I'd been asking myself for several months. I said, "Dad, no one is making me go. I just believe I have to go! If I don't, all the things I teach others about evangelism will be nothing more than empty words. How can I ask people if they would be willing to die for Christ if I'm not? How can I, when I'm speaking at a missions conference, ask, 'Would you go anywhere God has called you?' if I'm not willing? And, Dad, how can I say I trust God if I'm not willing to show Him by putting my life on the line? I have to trust God."

On my flight to Pakistan, I opened my Bible to Psalm 56:3-4.

When I am afraid,
I will trust in you.
In God, whose word I praise,
in God I trust; I will not be afraid.
What can mortal man do to me?

I needed to see that promise from God, and I clung to those words for the next eight days.

I recited them when I heard that members of the committee organizing the campaign had received death threats.

I reminded myself of God's promise when I discovered that the day before I arrived, a truck full of men with machine guns had pulled up in front of the chairman's home, parked for thirty minutes, and pointed their guns at the house.

I held those words close to my heart when one of the men protecting me said moments before I walked onto the platform, "If you say the wrong thing tonight, our enemies are here, and they will kill you on the spot."

Looking back at that experience brings joy to my soul. I was afraid, and I trusted in God. Not only did God protect me, He also did a great work in that stadium each night as thousands came to Christ.

Today God comes to you and says the same words He said to me: "Trust Me. When you are afraid, trust Me. In your day-to-day life, trust Me. Do not put your trust in your friends or your bank account or your wisdom or anything else. Put your trust in Me."

In God we *can* trust.

Chapter 2

IN GOD WE CAN TRUST

One summer my oldest son came to me asking the "Bank of Dad" to open its doors one more time. Ben's request was simple: "Dad, I need $200."

Now that petition took a quantum leap from Ben needing five bucks to go see a movie with a friend, and I had a feeling the "bank" was not going to approve his withdrawal. Curiosity got the best of me though, so I asked what he was going to buy with this huge sum of money.

"Blades!"

Ah, in-line skates. And not just any skates. The biggest, baddest, most extreme blades you could find. With these skates Ben was convinced he would go faster, jump higher, grind longer, and break more bones than ever before possible.

I thought about his request and got an ingenious idea. "Ben, you are going to get the money for those blades," I said. His eyes lit up. "But I am not going to give you the money. You are going to earn the money." His eyes rolled back into his head.

Exasperated, Ben wanted to know how he was going to earn

$200, especially since he needed the money that very day. So I dove into my moneymaking strategy with Ben and laid out the plan that was going to make him rich and keep me out of Chapter 11.

The strategy was simple: I was going to teach Ben how to mow lawns.

"You have to be kidding, Dad," was his not-so-warm response.

I replied, "Trust me, Ben." So we pushed the mower out of the garage and to our front yard and began phase 1 of my strategy—a lesson on lawn mowing. I showed Ben how to put gas in the mower, how to start it, how to take the catcher off, and how to stop it in an emergency. Then I started the mower and showed him the different directions you could mow and the patterns you could make.

We then moved to the backyard, and I let him loose on the lawn. He did a great job and was now ready for phase 2. "Now, Ben, we are going to go into the house and use the computer to make a flyer promoting Ben's Lawn Mowing Service."

"Are you sure, Dad?"

"Trust me, Ben."

The flyer looked great, informing the prospective customer who Ben Owens was and how well he could mow lawns and listing the prices. We were ready to make some cash.

Outside, the summer sun was heating things up. Ben now eyed me with the "OK, Dad, what next?" look. It was time for the third and final phase—one that would be forever embedded in Owens family history.

"Ben, I want you to take these flyers and the lawn mower, and I want you to go house to house. When you knock on the door, hand the person a flyer and ask if he or she would like the lawn mowed."

"Are you sure, Dad?"

"Trust me, Ben, trust me."

Off he went. About an hour later I heard the lawn mower clattering down the sidewalk. I eagerly went out to meet my new entrepreneur and immediately saw that he'd had a setback.

"Dad, this isn't working! Not one person has asked me to mow their lawn, and it's getting hot out here."

It was time for a pep talk. "Ben, this is your first day, and you've only been working for an hour. It takes time, but it will happen. You *will* make money today."

After a quick drink, Ben was ready to go again. As I watched him trudge down the street once more, I prayed, "O God, give him one paying customer today."

Forty-five minutes passed before I heard the lawn mower again. Never being a person of great faith, I was almost afraid to go outside. To my delight, I noticed Ben had sweat pouring down his face and little green flakes stuck to his clothes. Just then he raised his arm, waved a twenty dollar bill at me, and shouted, "Dad, you're a genius. You were right. And I have another customer waiting for me!" Oh, the joy of being a genius in the eyes of your children!

As I pulled out a lawn chair and sat down to enjoy the sun, I started thinking about what I'd said repeatedly to Ben throughout the morning: "Trust me, Ben." That's what I wanted him to do. I wanted him to see that he could trust me in his new business endeavor.

Ben earned the desired $200 that summer and bought the inline skates he wanted. The next summer he made $600 and bought his first guitar. Why? Because he trusted my advice.

Ben's trust makes me think about the many times the Lord has come to me with that same request: "Trust Me, Dan, trust Me." So many times He has encouraged me to trust Him through His Word, though His Spirit, and through His faithfulness. And so many times I have done just the opposite and have been swallowed up by worry and fear. The prophet Jeremiah wrote:

This is what the LORD *says:*
"Cursed is the one who trusts in man,
who depends on flesh for his strength
and whose heart turns away from the Lord."

JEREMIAH 17:5

Whatever advice men and women give pales in comparison to the wisdom the Lord promises us. Jeremiah said it so well:

This is what the LORD *says:*
"Let not the wise man boast of his wisdom
or the strong man boast of his strength
or the rich man boast of his riches,
but let him who boasts boast about this:
that he understands and knows me,
that I am the LORD, *who exercises kindness,*
justice and righteousness on earth,
for in these I delight."

JEREMIAH 9:23-24

Just as I feel a sense of joy when I reflect on Ben's response to my advice a few summers ago, I know it brings God great joy when I trust Him with my life.

But it can't be that simple, can it? I mean, is God reliable? Can I really count on Him when things don't go as planned? Does He really look out for my best interests? How do I know He won't mess up my life?

We may not like to admit it, but those thoughts have hounded most of us. I'm ashamed to say, I too have questioned whether God can really be trusted.

Instead of feeling guilty and sweeping our questions into the corners of our minds, let's address the issue. Can God be trusted? Although many things in the Bible remain unclear, the Scriptures provide us with ample proof of God's trustworthiness. We can examine many clear-cut examples of

God's nature and His being. (One of the greatest things you can do if you are struggling with worry and doubt is to do a personal study on the attributes of God. Your local Christian bookstore would be a great place to find books on God's nature and character.)

Let's start with the very names of God Himself.

The two most commonly used names found in the Bible for the Lord are *Elohim* and *Yahweh*. Biblical scholars translated *Yahweh* as "Lord" and *Elohim* as "God."

In its most simple form *Yahweh* or *Lord* means "self-existent." This means God doesn't need anything else in order to live. His life doesn't come from another source because He is life. He doesn't need food or air or water or even purpose to live, because He created all those things. Because He is self-existent, He doesn't rely on anyone or anything. Nothing can stop Him from providing us with everything we need. He can be trusted for our daily provisions.

The other most frequently used name for the Lord is *Elohim* or *God*. Whereas *Yahweh* speaks more of who God is, *Elohim* draws attention to His power. We find this word for God used well over 2,500 times in the Bible, with thirty-two mentions found in the first chapter of Genesis alone.

"In the beginning God [Elohim] created the heavens and the earth." This name for God embraces the idea of a *creative governing power with omnipotence and sovereignty*. The power of God called all of creation into existence, and by His sovereignty He rules over it every single day.

Not surprisingly we also find *Elohim* or its root *El* ("strength") used throughout the book of Psalms, which often discusses the power of God in creation.

> *The heavens declare the glory of God;*
> *the skies proclaim the work of his hands.*
> *Day after day they pour forth speech;*

night after night they display knowledge.
There is no speech or language
where their voice is not heard.
Their voice goes out into all the earth,
their words to the ends of the world.

19:1-4

In this passage the psalmist praises God, who is all-powerful and sovereign, for the universe and all that it tells us about Him.

I like how *The Living Bible* paraphrases this same passage:

The heavens are telling the glory of God,
they are a marvelous display of his craftsmanship.
Day and night they keep on telling about God.
Without a word or sound, silent in the skies,
their message reaches out to all the world.

The skies reveal so much about God. While preaching at the Metropolitan Tabernacle in London, Charles Spurgeon said, "A survey of our solar system has the tendency to moderate the pride of man and promote humility."

Considering all the astronomical discoveries of the past several decades, I am amazed that man is not more in awe of his Creator. Instead, the public is drawn more toward aliens, Area 51, and out-of-control meteors crashing into earth. Others behave like those discoveries are as commonplace as dish soap.

Not me! Even as a boy I was intrigued by the stars and gazed for long hours at the evening's canopy of light. I still stand in wonder when I see photographs of other galaxies and gaseous clouds in distant space.

I live with my family in San Diego, not far from the famous Palomar Observatory. With telescopes like the one at Palomar and other powerful instruments that scientists use, we have learned some amazing things about our universe.

For instance, we know that Earth sits in a magnificent galaxy called the Milky Way, along with billions of other stars and planets. Have you ever seen a picture of the Milky Way with the arrow pointing to our beloved planet? Earth looks like a tiny grain of sand on the beach. Let's assume for a moment that you wanted to travel from one end of our galaxy to the other at the speed of light. Light travels at the incredible speed of 186,000 miles per second, or roughly 700 million miles per hour. That means you would need 100,000 years to travel from one end of our galaxy to the other.

Would you like to visit another galaxy? Our closest neighboring galaxy is called Andromeda, or as the scientists call it, NGC 224. This galaxy contains 200 billion suns and untold mysteries and is two million light-years (the distance light can travel in a year) away from us. How far away is that? Andromeda is 13 quintillion miles away. That's a 13 followed by 18 zeros. If we boarded Voyager 2, one of the fastest unmanned spacecrafts we have invented to date, traveling to Andromeda would take 150 billion years!

Next time you're outside at night, gaze into the cup of the Big Dipper. Scientists estimate that more than one million galaxies occupy the space within the four points of those stars.

Carl Sagan, the late astronomer and physicist, wrote in his book *Cosmos* that enough known galaxies exist in the universe for every man, woman, and child on Planet Earth to own several each. Billions of known galaxies exist, and as we use technology such as the Hubble telescope, it's likely millions more will be discovered.

Space, so incredibly vast, shows that God, Elohim, the creative governing power of omnipotence and sovereignty, is infinite.

Not only have we discovered vast distances in space, but we also know about immense bodies in the heavens that cannot be appreciated with the human eye. It has been calculated that the sun, if it were hollow, could hold 1.3 million Earths. The star

Antares could hold 64 million of our suns. Far away in the constellation of Hercules is a star that could hold 100 million Antares. And we know of other stars that are bigger still.

Or think about this: We are spinning on Earth's axis at 1,000 miles per hour, hurtling on our orbit through space at 67,000 miles per hour, and we don't even feel it.

Have these few examples from the heavens demonstrated to you that the very name of God, Elohim, the one who "created the heavens and the earth," has one exploding message for us? "Trust Me!" God says to us. "If I can create an unlimited universe, if I can bring into existence the laws of nature, if I can hold the stars in space, if I can stop the sun from moving closer and burning up the earth or moving farther away and freezing the earth, if I can do all these things, then can't you trust Me?"

"God . . . is the blessed controller of all things" (1 Timothy 6:15, *Phillips*). God is worthy of our trust. To say that we cannot trust Him is to place ourselves in the position of God. If I do not, cannot, or will not trust God with my life, then I am no longer worshiping Him. I have returned to idol worship and me worship.

What person in his right mind would say to God, "I don't trust You"? Yet we say it every day through our actions, attitudes, and words. Maybe it's time for you and me to take a walk late at night, look up at the stars, and remember in whom we are to place our trust.

Most of us remember the story of Job in the Old Testament. In the eyes of the world, Job had it all! This very wealthy man owned 7,000 sheep, 3,000 camels, 500 yoke of oxen, and 500 donkeys. He also was blessed with a large family, having seven sons and three daughters. Of more value than his wealth, Job was a man of integrity, and the Bible tells us that God was fully pleased with him.

After a dialogue with Satan, God decided to put Job under the microscope of suffering—not because of personal sin in Job's life but to demonstrate the genuineness of his faith. And suffer he did! He lost his flocks and his wealth. He lost family members and friends. He lost his wife's respect and trust when she told Job to "Curse God and die." How would you like your spouse to comfort you with those words? She must have been a real blessing!

During his time of suffering, people gave advice to Job. Some of the counsel was good, and some, probably most, was way off. But through it all, Job held on to the belief that God was sovereign and knew best.

Yet, in time Job began to doubt and question God—something we all have done and may be doing today. Job began to ask why. "Why, God? Why this, God? Why now, God? Why?"

After many such questions, God spoke to Job personally. He had listened to the counsel Job's friends gave and the defiant words of Job's wife, but now God spoke. Job 38—42 gives a brilliant account of the conversation, mostly one-sided, that God had with Job then. Let me highlight bits of that conversation for you.

Job 38:1-3 sets up the dialogue:

> *Then the* LORD *answered Job out of the storm. He said:*
> *"Who is this that darkens my counsel*
> *with words without knowledge?*
> *Brace yourself like a man;*
> *I will question you,*
> *and you shall answer me."*

Imagine you are driving down the road, complaining to God as we all sometimes do, and all of a sudden you hear a loud voice saying, "Brace yourself like a man; I will question you, and you shall answer Me." I would lose control of my car, my bladder, and my right mind! Job must have stopped in his tracks when he heard the thunderous voice of God.

Let's see what kind of questions God asked of Job.

> *"Where were you when I laid the earth's foundations?*
> *Tell me, if you understand.*
> *Who marked off its dimensions?*
> *Surely you know!*
> *Who stretched a measuring line across it?*
> *On what were its footings set,*
> *or who laid its cornerstone—*
> *while the morning stars sang together*
> *and all the angels shouted for joy?"*
>
> JOB 38:4-7

God began to question Job about creation. Did you catch the sarcasm when God made the statement, "Surely you know!" Of course Job didn't have the answer. But God pressed on with His questions in verses 18-21:

> *"Have you comprehended the vast*
> *expanses of the earth?*
> *Tell me if you know all this.*
> *What is the way to the abode of light?*
> *And where does darkness reside?*
> *Can you take them to their places?*
> *Do you know the paths to their dwellings?*
> *Surely you know, for you were already born!*
> *You have lived so many years!"*

I can only imagine the emotion Job was experiencing. You can feel the heat being turned up as God again probed Job with questions tinged with sarcasm. I don't think God used this tactic to demean Job. Job knew God and knew better than to lose patience with God. I'm sure if we behaved like Job, the Lord would ask us those very same questions.

Further on in chapter 38 God asked Job about the heavens:

"Can you bind the beautiful Pleiades?
Can you loose the cords of Orion?
Can you bring forth the constellations
in their seasons
or lead out the Bear [or Leo] with its cubs?
Do you know the laws of the heavens?
Can you set up God's dominion over the earth?"

VERSES 31-33

God continued to move through His list of questions all through chapters 38 and 39. At last we see hope of a reprieve when God invited Job to answer Him in the first few verses of chapter 40.

The LORD *said to Job:*
"Will the one who contends with
the Almighty correct him?
Let him who accuses God answer him!"

VERSES 1-2

Have you ever thought of your complaining as accusations against God?

Then Job answered the LORD*:*
"I am unworthy—how can I reply to you?
I put my hand over my mouth.
I spoke once, but I have no answer—
twice, but I will say no more."

VERSES 3-5

Job responded like any of us would. He fell on his face before the Lord and cried out that he was unworthy and that he had spoken of things he knew nothing about.

God kept asking Job for the answers to questions because Job had acted as if he knew so much. But as God questioned him, Job began to see his life from God's perspective.

Sometimes we feel like we know it all, or at least a good portion of it. We think we know what's best. We're sure we have the answers. But we are seeing only a grain of sand in the ocean of God's eternal purposes. Job was just beginning to realize that fact when God spoke again.

> *"Brace yourself like a man;*
> *I will question you,*
> *and you shall answer me."*
> VERSE 7

Not again?

Yes, God came back with more questions, and Job again couldn't answer them.

When you've finished reading this chapter, you might want to put down this book, pick up your Bible, and read the last five chapters of Job (38—42). You will see that God gives Job a sixty-six question test covering a range of subjects—geology, botany, biology, zoology, astronomy, natural laws, physical laws, and a host of other sciences. When Job received his score back, he discovered that out of sixty-six questions, he did not answer one correctly. *Not one.*

Job failed the oral test. So would I. So would you. However, Job did learn the lesson—namely, God's desire or purpose for each of us during times of testing. We can fail the test, but we must not fail to learn the lesson.

In the last chapter of the book, Job recites to the Lord the essence of the lesson he'd learned:

> *Then Job replied to the LORD:*
> *"I know that you can do all things;*
> *no plan of yours can be thwarted.*
> *You asked, 'Who is this that obscures*
> *my counsel without knowledge?'*
> *Surely I spoke of things I did not understand,*

things too wonderful for me to know.
You said, 'Listen now, and I will speak;
I will question you, and you shall answer me.'
My ears had heard of you
but now my eyes have seen you.
Therefore I despise myself
and repent in dust and ashes."

42:1-6

Job had experienced God for himself and had learned the lesson God wanted to teach him: *It is better to know God than to know all the answers.*

God's desire through His dealings with Job was for Job to trust Him. Did you notice that God never answered one of Job's questions? He didn't have to. He was not obligated to. God knew what He was doing even when, from our human perspective, He allowed Job to go through a living hell.

Like Job, we will never know all the answers, all the reasons for our trials and afflictions, but you and I can know God, and that is what really matters. To try to understand the reasons for all our dilemmas is fruitless. We know that sometimes we bring troubles on ourselves by our disobedience, but other times trials come out of nowhere, and these are the most difficult to accept. We have to remember that God wants us to focus on Him, not on the answers to our questions.

As I write these words, I am far from home in a beautiful area of Pennsylvania, speaking at an evangelistic festival. Under the leadership of a twenty-seven-year-old pastor, the churches in the area got together and decided it was time to reach out to their community with the Gospel. Money was raised, musical artists were booked, sound systems and lighting were rented, people were trained, and the believers began to pray.

The first night of the festival, everything was in place. The high school football field looked like a miniature Woodstock with the stage set up, lighting in place, concession stands selling burgers, and people playing on the grass. The only problem was rain. Outdoor events and precipitation do not go well together. We made it in spite of the weather, but attendance was rather low.

As the second evening approached, we all hoped the weather would be more kind. I arrived early at the high school to pray with some of the committee, and the sun was shining. Things were looking brighter. Steve Camp opened that night's program, leading a 150-voice choir, and the crowd began to grow. Also growing in the distance was a huge storm.

As Steve sang, I noticed that the lightning flashes were moving closer. As Steve and the choir were finishing and I moved to step onto the platform, the young pastor came to me and said, "The storm is headed right toward us, and it's going to be a bad one. But I have faith that it will miss us. So go ahead and start preaching."

Although I am from California and am used to earthquakes, I did not want to experience a lightning storm up close. I answered, "We're not going to presume on God. The report says the storm is coming this way, and the last thing you want is for someone to get hurt in the storm or even struck by lightning. I'm going to close in prayer and tell everyone to go home."

Less than two minutes after I had dismissed the crowd, the predicted storm arrived. Lightning began to strike all around us, the rain began to pelt us horizontally, and everyone was running for cover. Then the wind picked up to 80 miles per hour, which is when the real trouble started. The gusts hit the stage with such force that they lifted eight 300-pound speakers into the air and dropped them off the stage. One speaker crashed into a monitor board. The wind ripped off the stage and twisted the metal trusses that held the lights like spaghetti. The choir director was blown off the stage and had to be rushed to the hospital with broken ribs. The wind and driving rain leveled everything.

Within twenty minutes the storm was over, and it looked like the festival was over too.

Why would God allow something as good as an evangelistic festival to be thwarted and the equipment destroyed and some of His servants seriously injured? Didn't God know that I was going to be preaching the Gospel and that hundreds of people could be saved? How could He allow such a disaster?

I have to be honest. I asked those very questions two nights ago. I still don't know the answers, but it has been exciting to see the leaders work with what they had and continue with the event. It has been interesting to see all three network news stations report on the bizarre events that took place. The Christians here received free publicity beyond their wildest dreams, and last night more than 3,000 people attended the festival—a massive number for this area.

The Old Testament poet and hymn-writer Asaph wrote in Psalm 73:25-26:

> *Whom have I in heaven but you?*
> *And earth has nothing I desire besides you.*
> *My flesh and my heart may fail,*
> *but God is the strength of my heart*
> *and my portion forever.*

God taught Job to trust Him, and He continues to teach us that very same lesson. We may have the attitude "In God we trust, but only as a last resort," but God is working to change that in us. He wants us to trust Him from the moment we climb out of bed until we close our eyes at night.

Why do we rage such a battle against childlike trust? The next five chapters will discuss why most of us struggle to put our trust in God.

Chapter 3

IT'S MORE SERIOUS THAN YOU THINK

Oswald Chambers wrote, "All worry and anxiety come from the fact that we have calculated without God." Sleepless nights, eating disorders, and days without joy follow efforts to work out solutions to our problems, real or imagined, through our own wisdom or strength. Once we take our eyes off the Lord and focus on the problem facing us, the cancer of fear begins to take over our entire personality.

Fear and faith cannot coexist. I speak here not of the fear of the Lord commended in Proverbs and elsewhere in the Scriptures, but a fear of men, failure, suffering, etc. Fear will stop you in your tracks and will keep you from seeing God do the miraculous. Fear will keep you from experiencing God as He unleashes His power in your life. Fear will rob you of the joy of knowing that your loving Father is watching over you.

We often think that a lack of faith in God is not all that serious. Compared to adultery or idolatry or even gossip, faithlessness just does not seem that alarming. But faithlessness offends God. When was the last time you got on your knees and confessed to the Lord that your worrying was the result of a lack of faith in Him? Have you ever asked the Lord to forgive your sin of fear and unbelief? It's too easy to excuse our lack of faith as mere weakness or to laughingly say that faith is not our gift; but the Lord does not share our flippancy in the matter. There is an incredible account in the book of Numbers in which God shows us clearly the importance He places on our trust in Him.

Numbers 13—14 tells about the children of Israel finally coming to the end of their exodus from Egypt and their wilderness wanderings. The Lord had led them through the desert in a miraculous way, showing His great power and kindness at every turn. It was now time to settle down and enjoy the peace and rest that would come from being in the place God had prepared for them. They were about to be given a huge amount of land that they could call "home," something they had not known for a long, long time. Understandably, the journey had not been without its problems—moving more than a million people over a great distance and through difficult terrain isn't easy. But now there was to be joy in the camp.

This story always reminds me of taking a family trip by car and the little voices from the backseat continually asking, "Are we there yet?" I can only imagine how sick of that question Moses had become! Can you imagine how many times he heard, "I'm hungry. Can we stop and get something to eat?" Easier said than done. Moses couldn't just pull over to McDonald's and order a million Big Macs, fries, and shakes. And even if he could have, the people who preferred Taco Bell would have complained. The children of Israel had become experts at the art of grumbling, and the Lord had taken note of it. But now as they came to the end of their journey all those problems seemed to have been forgotten.

But the excitement must have been a bit overshadowed when the host of people realized there was one more hurdle to overcome before they could take occupancy of the land. They had to remove several barbaric civilizations. Can you imagine someone giving you a home for free, but the people currently living in it don't want to leave? It's yours—all you have to do is throw them out. Right! The Israelites must have felt the same way. "We've traveled through the desert for two years, believing the land was ours, and now you tell us it's occupied by other civilizations that we have to fight against and destroy before we can make ourselves at home? Thanks for nothing!" And don't forget that the civilizations that occupied the land were highly advanced and well armed. The Canaanites had been around for more than 600 years and had well-fortified cities, with established governments and languages. The Israelites didn't even know anything about some of these people groups.

As the Israelites came to Kadesh, Moses commanded them to set up camp so that from there he could send out spies into the land who would then bring back a report about its beauty—and its obstacles. One spy was taken from each tribe. In modern-day military vernacular, this was a reconnaissance mission, one that was making the people a bit nervous. But Moses had a different perspective on what God was about to do.

Why? "The LORD said to Moses, 'Send some men to explore the land of Canaan, *which I am giving to the Israelites*. From each ancestral tribe send one of its leaders'" (Numbers 13:1). The Lord was quite clear that *He* was going to be the one who would give them the land. In an earlier account the Lord had given even greater detail—what He expected from Israel in the process, and what He was going to give to them once they accomplished this task.

> *"See, I am sending an angel ahead of you to guard you along the way and to bring you to the place I have prepared. Pay attention to him and listen to what he says. Do not rebel against him; he will not forgive your rebellion, since my Name is in him. If you listen carefully to what*

he says and do all that I say, I will be an enemy to your enemies and will oppose those who oppose you. My angel will go ahead of you and bring you into the land of the Amorites, Hittites, Perizzites, Canaanites, Hivites and Jebusites, and I will wipe them out. Do not bow down before their gods or worship them or follow their practices. You must demolish them and break their sacred stones to pieces. Worship the LORD *your God, and his blessing will be on your food and water. I will take away sickness from among you, and none will miscarry or be barren in your land. I will give you a full life span."*

EXODUS 23:20-26

You can feel the awesome love and compassion that the Lord was ready to pour upon His people. God was giving to Moses a picture of the good life that was awaiting them in the new land that He had promised to Abraham centuries before. I'm sure Moses was excited to pass on this vision to his people as they made their two-year trek to this pivotal time and place.

The Lord continued in Exodus 23 to tell how He was going to drive out those people who had no desire to leave and give up their land: "I will send my terror ahead of you and throw into confusion every nation you encounter. I will make all your enemies turn their backs and run. I will send the hornet ahead of you to drive the Hivites, Canaanites and Hittites out of your way. But I will not drive them out in a single year, because the land would become desolate and the wild animals too numerous for you. Little by little I will drive them out before you, until you have increased enough to take possession of the land" (verses 27-30).

God could not have made it more clear! "Moses, I will go before you and give you this land." All Moses and the people had to do was listen to the Lord and obey His commands. And His first command was to send out a recon party.

Numbers 13 lists the names of the team that went in to spy

out the land, but the two central characters in this story are Joshua and Caleb. God had told Moses to pick a *leader* from each tribe, and Joshua and Caleb proved to be leaders in more ways than one. I want to especially focus our attention on Caleb and his impact on the subsequent history of Israel.

The twelve spies were sent into the land to bring back a report to Moses and the people. The mission, which took forty days to complete, had mixed results. "They came back to Moses and Aaron and the whole Israelite community at Kadesh in the Desert of Paran" (Numbers 13:26). This was not a private meeting. The spies shared their information with the entire nation because Moses was confident that the Lord would keep His word and give them the land. He had nothing to fear. Any news would be good news because the Lord was going to fight their battles for them and give them the good life.

It was time for the news they had been waiting to hear. "There they reported to them and to the whole assembly and showed them the fruit of the land. They gave Moses this account: 'We went into the land to which you sent us, and it does flow with milk and honey! Here is its fruit.'" So far so good! "Milk and honey" was symbolic of an overabundance of food. We would use the phrase "What a spread!" or "Enough for an army!" The Lord had kept His word—the land was very good indeed.

Now came the defining moment. The spies continued, "But the people who live there are powerful, and the cities are fortified and very large. We even saw descendants of Anak there. The Amalekites live in the Negev; the Hittites, Jebusites and Amorites live in the hill country; and the Canaanites live near the sea and along the Jordan" (verses 28-29).

Moses probably thought, "Yeah, so what?" He knew those people were there because the Lord had told him. But the assembly as a whole began to have a problem with the scenario. To learn that the descendants of Anak (giants) were walking around was a little too much for them. They began to get cold feet about the whole thing. Fear began to take control of their personalities and their decision-making processes. Have you ever experienced that? You work hard to accomplish some task until a new bit of information is inserted into the equation, and your excitement turns into fear. My sons wanted to fly to England with me, until they found out they'd have to fly over the ocean for several hours. Fear dispelled their excitement.

But in this portion of biblical history one man didn't take God out of his calculations, and thus he was able to set aside his fear and focus on his faith. "Then Caleb silenced the people before Moses and said, 'We should go up and take possession of the land, for we can certainly do it'" (verse 30).

A DIFFERENT VIEW

The twelve spies all saw the same things over the forty days. They all agreed there was plenty of good food in the land. There was no argument that this would be a wonderful place to live. The difference came in how the spies viewed the people living there and whether or not the Israelites could remove them against their will. Caleb put God in the equation because God had already put Himself there. No doubt Caleb remembered the words of the Lord that were passed along by Moses. God said He was "giving" the land to them. The Lord had promised He would send His angel before them to fight their battles. Caleb remembered, and Caleb believed God. He put his faith and his trust in God and didn't let the obvious circumstances make him afraid.

The Lord was thrilled with the faith of Caleb and Joshua but was furious at the doubts of the ten other spies and the assembly that day. Because of their unbelief, God banished them to forty years of wandering in the desert, where they would eventually perish without ever stepping foot in the land He had set aside for them.

How can we say God is not offended by our sin of unbelief?

How can we think our skepticism toward His promises will go unnoticed? Read carefully the words of Hebrews 3:12: "See to it, brothers, that none of you has a sinful, unbelieving heart that turns away from the living God."

I wonder how many times I have in effect called God a liar because I didn't believe Him. *Liar* is a strong word, but the fact is, when God has spoken to you and me through His Word and we choose not to believe Him, we are calling Him a liar! Think about that! The audacity of God's creation standing toe to toe with Him and calling Him a liar—it's inconceivable. He knows no sin, He is holy and just, He gives us our very life—and yet we dare say to Him, "I don't believe You!" Whether we say it with fear-filled words like the children of Israel did or just live it out by our actions, it is clear we do not believe God. I shudder at the number of times I have been guilty of this greatest of sins.

Now, this was not the first time the Israelites had allowed fear to cloud their thinking. In fact, there were numerous occasions when God had all but turned His back on them because they refused to believe Him. Here was God, looking out for their best interests, taking them out of captivity, providing for their every need on their journey, proving His power and love every step of the way, and they still would not believe. On one occasion they were angry because there was no water to drink (Exodus 17). They began to grumble against Moses and actually started insulting God by accusing Him of bringing them out into the desert to die of thirst. Then, as if that were not bad enough, they began to ask if the Lord was really alive! The Bible says God was exasperated with their attitude.

Has fear ever overcome you to the extent that you didn't believe God was really with you? I confess that for years fear dictated too many of my decisions. I lived in dread of "what if," those deepest fears that gnaw at us even when things are going well. What if I lose my job, what if the economy goes bad, what if I get cancer, what if my kids do drugs, what if my wife (or husband) leaves me, what if I don't have enough money when I retire, what if there's a nuclear war, what if . . . ?

After being in the ministry for more than twenty years, I was struggling with what to do with my life. I had served the Lord for ten years on church staffs and then another ten years with the Luis Palau Evangelistic Association. My dad sensed my restlessness and asked me a question: "Dan, if you could do anything you wanted, what would you do?" I knew the answer before he even finished. I told him I would love to form my own ministry and be free to preach and speak whenever someone invited me to do so. "So what's keeping you from doing that?" Dad asked.

For weeks that question rattled around in my soul. I knew what I wanted to do and, even more importantly, I knew what God had gifted me to do. Why could I not step out in faith and begin a new ministry of evangelism and renewal?

I will never forget the day that God showed me what was keeping me from taking a new journey with Him. I was full of fear! Through the years friends had praised me for how I'd planned so well for my lifework and family. I did very few things without weighing all the options and counting the cost. I was always proud of this until God showed me that my actions were actually motivated by fear. Everything I did was motivated by fear. I had fear about the future, fear about finances, fear about vacations, fear about my family. I lived in fear, just like the children of Israel.

I cannot tell you the joy that filled my soul when I got down on my knees and confessed to God that I'd been sinning against Him for years. I asked God to help me overcome my fear and to live by faith in Him. It was only after I confessed my sin that God gave me the desire and courage to step out in total faith and begin Eternity Minded Ministries.

Caleb believed God would keep His word. He had watched

the Lord do great things over the past several years as God led the Hebrews to this monumental occasion. Caleb was there when the plagues were given as a sign to Pharaoh. He watched God open the sea for Israel. He saw God provide manna from heaven and quail to eat until everyone was full. He saw God lead them as a pillar of fire by night and a cloud during the day. He saw God bring forth water from a rock. Caleb believed nothing was too big for God to do, especially when God had already said He was going to do it.

A DIFFERENT VOICE

Caleb had spoken words of faith and courage that brought glory to God, but as happens so often, many people did not share his views. In fact, only Joshua was on his side. The ten other spies succumbed to fear. "'We can't attack those people; they are stronger than we are,' they reported. And they spread among the Israelites a bad report about the land they had explored. They said, 'The land we explored devours those living in it. All the people we saw there are of great size. We saw the Nephilim there (the descendants of Anak come from the Nephilim). We seemed like grasshoppers in our own eyes, and we looked the same to them'" (Numbers 13:31-33).

Not exactly a speech to rouse the troops for action! With their words the ten spies demoralized the assembly and ignited the fears that were already smoldering within the people, making it look like Joshua and Caleb had misread the situation altogether.

By that evening the fire of unbelief had grown into a raging inferno. "That night all the people of the community raised their voices and wept aloud. All the Israelites grumbled against Moses and Aaron, and the whole assembly said to them, 'If only we had died in Egypt! Or in this desert! Why is the LORD bringing us to this land only to let us fall by the sword? Our wives and children will be taken as plunder. Wouldn't it better for us to go back to Egypt?' And they said to each other, 'We should choose a leader and go back to Egypt'" (Numbers 14:1-4).

If not for the fact that unbelief is so serious, their response could be seen as humorous. After all they had seen the Lord do, and after hearing from Moses that the Lord was going to send an angel into the land ahead of them to fight for them, they let fear rule the day. They accused God of bringing them there to die by the sword! They accused God of constructing a plan that would bring their families to ruin! They accused God of not knowing what He was doing in choosing Moses to lead them! Once again they were calling God a liar.

Moses, Aaron, Joshua, and Caleb knew this would not go well with the Lord. They feared this could be the last straw. With passion and pleading they stepped in to try to keep the Israelites from putting themselves under the Lord's judgment.

> *Then Moses and Aaron fell facedown in front of the whole Israelite assembly gathered there. Joshua son of Nun and Caleb son of Jephunneh, who were among those who had explored the land, tore their clothes and said to the entire Israelite assembly, "The land we passed through and explored is exceedingly good. If the* LORD *is pleased with us, he will lead us into that land, a land flowing with milk and honey, and will give it to us. Only do not rebel against the* LORD. *And do not be afraid of the people of the land, because we will swallow them up. Their protection is gone, but the* LORD *is with us. Do not be afraid of them."*
>
> NUMBERS 14:5-9

But this appeal to common sense and spiritual sensitivity was to no avail. "But the whole assembly talked about stoning them" (verse 10). Can you imagine?

Now God had heard enough. "Then the glory of the LORD

appeared at the Tent of the Meeting to all the Israelites. The LORD said to Moses, 'How long will these people treat me with contempt? How long will they refuse to *believe* in me, in spite of all the miraculous signs I have performed among them?'" (verses 10-11, italics added). God then said He was going to destroy them because of their unbelief.

Does God consider an unbelieving heart to be a trite or petty thing? Does God allow us to spread fear, doubt, and negativism without consequences?

The ten spies were confident as they stirred up the assembly. They were sure they were right and the other two were missing the boat. Since the people sided with them, they were certain they weren't wrong in their evaluation of the circumstances. They undoubtedly felt their words were righteous. But God judged them for their sin, condemning the nation of Israel to wander in the desert for another forty years. Rather than destroying the assembly, the Lord gave them exactly what they asked for, as expressed through Moses and Aaron:

> *"'As surely as I live,' declares the LORD, 'I will do to you the very things I heard you say: In this desert your bodies will fall—every one of you twenty years old or more who was counted in the census and who has grumbled against me. Not one of you will enter the land I swore with uplifted hand to make your home, except Caleb son of Jephunneh and Joshua son of Nun. As for your children that you said would be taken as plunder, I will bring them in to enjoy the land you have rejected. But you—your bodies will fall in this desert.'"*
>
> NUMBERS 14:28-32

God held them accountable for the very words that had come from their mouths. Only Joshua and Caleb escaped God's judgment because they had a different view and a different voice.

A DIFFERENT VALUE

It is in times of crisis that we discover what we truly believe. Among the hundreds of thousands of people there in the desert, virtually only Caleb and Joshua put their faith in God. Pleased with Caleb's faith, God blessed him publicly and inscribed his name in the book of Numbers, never to be removed. The Israelites would die in the desert, God said. "'But because my servant Caleb has a different spirit and follows me wholeheartedly, I will bring him into the land he went to, and his descendants will inherit it'" (Numbers 14:24).

Caleb was going to live in the land that God wanted to give to all the Israelites. It was a shame that he would have to wander in the desert for forty years before he could collect on the promises of God. I would imagine, though, that he had just a little more bounce in his step during those years.

What was different about Caleb that made him view the land and its occupants differently from the rest of the assembly except for Joshua? Why would he speak positive words of faith in God when nearly everyone else wanted to choose new leaders and return to slavery in Egypt? God said Caleb had "a different spirit"; Caleb followed the Lord with his whole heart.

In 1990 I had the opportunity to minister with the Luis Palau Evangelistic Association throughout Romania. The country was experiencing new freedom after fifty years of Communist rule. Christians now not only could meet without fear in their churches, but also had the right to assemble in cultural halls and stadiums.

On my first visit to Romania I showed up in the dead of winter wearing West Coast clothing. After I collected my luggage at the Bucharest airport, I stepped outside into snow flurries and subzero temperature to find my contact, who I urgently prayed would actually be there. A slow-moving, bent-over old man walked toward me. He smiled, eyes twinkling, and asked if I was Dan Owens. My new Romanian friend was Pastor Ion Achim. Pastor Ion looked to be in his late sixties, with a body and a face that showed the wear and tear of life in a Communist country.

Pastor Ion insisted that I wear his big furry hat (something right out of *Dr. Zhivago*) and put on his coat. My objections were met by his stern insistence. His broken and accented English made him sound quite imposing. Besides, I didn't want to offend him, since he was much older than I and that would not be culturally correct.

I put on his hat and coat, noticing that they smelled like fuel, but the warmth they gave was much appreciated. Once we made it to his small car, I discovered the trunk and backseat were filled with containers of gasoline, necessary since they didn't have a gas station on every corner. The extra fuel was reassuring for a long trip, but it also made me quite nervous to know we were a moving Molotov cocktail!

Driving through the snowy streets, we began to share a bit about our lives. His eyes really sparkled with the joy of the Lord, and he became excited as he told me what God was doing in Romania. I began to ask him about his experiences as a minister in a Communist country. I heard stories about the wiretapping of phones, about listening devices placed in homes and churches, and about Christians imprisoned for their faith in Jesus Christ. It was then that I found out that Pastor Ion was not in his sixties but in fact was forty-two—only a few years older than I was. I was shocked that he looked so much older. Because of his preaching, Pastor Ion had been imprisoned for six years. There in that confinement, away from his family and his flock, he endured all the humiliation and pain that a harsh Communist system could dish out. His worn-out body gave witness to the years of persecution, but his sparkling eyes testified of his love for God. I felt like a spiritual pygmy in the presence of this man of God!

I had come to Bucharest to help Christians prepare for several crusades with Luis Palau. Pastor Ion wanted to do anything and everything to help these events succeed. One afternoon while we were alone drinking coffee to keep warm, his eyes filled with tears. "When I was in prison, I used to pray that the Gospel would someday be preached in the great stadiums of Romania," he said. "I did not know how it would happen, but I believed that God would one day let me see thousands of people coming to the stadiums to hear the good news of Jesus. God has answered my prayer!" With those words he began to weep with joy.

Here was a Caleb, a man with "a different spirit"! When others saw no spiritual hope for their country, no possible hope of slaying the giants in the land, Ion Achim believed God could do it. And God did it! Hundreds of thousands of people went to stadiums throughout Romania in 1990 and again in 1991 and heard about the love of God. Thousands opened their hearts to Jesus Christ, and hundreds of churches were planted. God was pleased by the faith of this man, and in contrast I was humbled by how little I knew of the power of God.

In *Apollo 13*, as the astronauts looked out the window at the moon they had come so close to touching, actor Tom Hanks asked that wonderful question, "Gentlemen, what are your intentions?" Were they going to stare out the window and talk of things that might have been, or were they going to get busy and find a way to bring their injured ship home? God our Father comes to us to ask that very same question. "Child of mine, what are your intentions?" Do I really want the Lord to work powerfully in my life? Do I truly want to forsake this world and follow God? Am I learning more about Him each day? Is it my intention to follow the Lord as closely as I can? Could it be that the reason I have such a hard time trusting God is because I really do not have any intention of doing so?

Too often we commit the sin of unbelief and give excuses for being so weak. The truth is, we don't want to believe God, we have no intention of allowing Him to be God. Like the Israelites in the desert, we call God a liar and cast Him aside.

But we need not despair or give up. We do not have to stay that way. Read on.

Chapter 4

I DID IT MY WAY

A counterfeiter from New York City decided a small town in the South would be the best place to pass off $18 bills. So he got into his shiny new car and headed toward Dixie. Passing through a town with only one store, he thought that would be a good place to start. Sure enough, the clerk behind the counter looked like someone from the land that time forgot. This was going to be easy.

"Can you change this for me please?" the city slicker said, handing the clerk an $18 bill.

The clerk looked closely at the bogus bill and then smiled. "Ah reckon I can change it for ya, mister," he said. "Did ya want two nines or three sixes?"

Proverbs 16:18 has withstood the test of time: "Pride goes before destruction, a haughty spirit before a fall." I have found that pride in any form directly conflicts with my ability to trust in God. It is impossible for me to harbor pride in its subtle forms of arrogance and conceit and also be able to rely on the power of God.

Isn't it interesting how easy we find it to openly confess some sins to God and people but not others? It's not uncommon to acknowledge our struggle with greed, jealousy, anger, even lust. We rarely, however, hear fellow believers confess their pride. How often do we say to a friend, "The Lord has shown me how arrogant I've become"? We find it much easier to confess our bitterness toward a brother or sister in Christ than to proclaim that we have harbored a spirit of arrogance.

Why is it so hard to admit our pride? *Everyone* struggles with this sin. Who hasn't been deceived into thinking that his motives were pure when in reality he was motivated by pride? But if a caring friend points out this sin in our lives, we're likely to react with anger. We don't want to be called a proud or arrogant person. We like to think of ourselves as humble and selfless even though we're surrounded by those who think more highly of themselves than they ought.

The Bible says our nemesis, Satan—then known as Lucifer—was thrown from the ranks of the inner courts of heaven because of his pride and his desire to dethrone God. In theory, though perhaps not in practice, we don't want to be guilty of the same sin to which God reacted with such sternness and finality. A sin so vile and hideous that it led God to forever ban Lucifer from heaven and to create a horrible place of torment for him and his followers. In Ezekiel 28 the Lord reveals the working of pride in the heart of Lucifer.

> *"You were the model of perfection,*
> *full of wisdom and perfect in beauty.*
> *You were in Eden,*
> *the garden of God;*
> *every precious stone adorned you:*
> *ruby, topaz, and emerald,*
> *chrysolite, onyx and jasper,*
> *sapphire, turquoise and beryl.*
> *Your settings and mountings were made of gold;*
> *on the day you were created they were prepared.*
> *You were anointed as a guardian cherub,*

for so I ordained you.
You were on the holy mount of God;
you walked among the fiery stones.
You were blameless in your ways
from the day you were created
till wickedness was found in you.
Through your widespread trade
you were filled with violence,
and you sinned.
So I drove you in disgrace from the mount of God,
and I expelled you, O guardian cherub,
from among the fiery stones.
Your heart became proud
on account of your beauty,
and you corrupted your wisdom
because of your splendor.
So I threw you to the earth;
I made a spectacle of you before kings."

VERSES 12-17

The created began to worship himself above his Creator. That is the essence of the sin of pride. Pride is self-worship! This can be ever so subtle, but it means symbolically removing God from His throne of worship and replacing Him with ourselves. I say symbolically because we cannot truly remove God from His sovereign position. From the Garden of Eden until now, the propensity of the human race has been to exalt itself above God.

Since the time of Adam's first sin, the Lord has clearly shown that the sin of pride will not be tolerated. In Proverbs 6:16-17 we see the seriousness of the sin of pride: "There are six things the LORD hates, seven that are detestable to him: haughty eyes . . ." Number one on God's list of the most detestable sins is pride. Why? Pride steals God's glory by exalting man. Pride says to God the Creator, "I don't need You." Pride is self-love. Pride is self-assertion. Pride does not trust God! "This is what the LORD says: 'Cursed is the one who trusts in man, who depends on flesh for his strength and whose heart turns away from the LORD'" (Jeremiah 17:5).

God knows that pride turned Lucifer away from Him and that our pride will do the same to us. In our arrogance we refuse the Lord's presence and power in our lives, saying to ourselves, "I can handle this situation on my own." But whether we recognize it or not, the Lord is continually moving us to a point of crisis where we will put our trust in Him, not only for our salvation, but for our daily needs.

INTELLECTUAL PRIDE

When I speak at men's retreats, I often hear stories of how the Lord brought men to a crisis point so they would put their trust in God. One man told an audience of 400 how the Lord had to take everything away from him—his cars, homes, even a private jet—in order to get his attention. He talked about the pride he took (which meant he was proud) in building his brokerage business from scratch. God took it away in a series of events that led him to faith in Jesus Christ as his Savior. Now this man who was once so proud of himself uses his time to bring other men to Jesus.

Intellectual pride says, "I am so smart. I can figure my life out. I can solve my own problems. I can do it all on my own." The successful broker was "a self-made man"—he started from nothing and built a prospering business. The problem with this attitude is, it's self-worship. There is no recognition that it is the Lord who gives a man the ability to earn money by providing the strength and the mind to do so. One stroke, one accident, one disease, and his ability to conquer the world is cut short. It can happen so quickly. The actor Christopher Reeves was paralyzed from the neck down when thrown from the horse he was riding. His life was immediately changed forever. I'm not saying that was because of pride, but just that any human life can change radically without a moment's notice.

In the parable of the rich fool, Jesus gave a warning against pride:

> *"Watch out! Be on your guard against all kinds of greed; a man's life does not consist in the abundance of his possessions." And he told them this parable: "The ground of a certain rich man produced a good crop. He thought to himself, 'What shall I do? I have no place to store my crops.' Then he said, 'This is what I will do. I will tear down my barns and build bigger ones, and there I will store all my grain and my goods. And I'll say to myself, "You have plenty of good things laid up for many years. Take life easy; eat, drink and be merry."' But God said to him, 'You fool! This very night your life will be demanded from you. Then who will get what you have prepared for yourself?' This is how it will be with anyone who stores up things for himself but is not rich toward God."*
>
> LUKE 12:15-21

This is the story of the classic American. Success is everything to him. He is a proud man who never gives a thought about anyone else's needs, but only his own advancement. He wants the good life of money, vacations, and early retirement. God is not opposed to our having money or enjoying life, but He is opposed to our hoarding money and using it for our own pleasure rather than for kingdom purposes. Even as followers of Jesus Christ we lose sight of the fact that God wants us to put our trust in Him and not in our accomplishments or our personal possessions.

You may be going through some difficulties at this time in your life. Could it be that the Lord is trying to get you to the point where you will say, "Lord, I need You"? Could it be that your pride is keeping you from fully trusting in God and fully experiencing Him? It's easy to praise God when all is going well, and we have plenty to eat, and there's a new car in the driveway, and we have the house we want and the money we think we need. But what happens when it's all taken away? Do we still praise God then? Do we trust Him and His plans for our lives?

PHYSICAL PRIDE

I can remember as a college student joining a gym to get in shape for football. One guy who worked there spent every available second looking at himself in the mirrors. He would spin around to see how he looked from different angles. While he was giving instruction to a client, he would be primping in the mirror. If someone was talking to him, he would be looking over the person's shoulder to make sure he looked just right. I was fascinated by this man's vanity.

One only has to go to the grocery store to realize that as a nation we are obsessed with appearance. Magazine cover after magazine cover puts perfectly sculpted men and flawless women on display—all imperfections are airbrushed out! No wonder the rest of us have such a hard time accepting ourselves! In Southern California where I live, the business of cosmetic surgery is growing by leaps and bounds.

There is nothing wrong with taking care of your body. The Lord even commands it: "Do you not know that your body is a temple of the Holy Spirit, who is in you, whom you have received from God? You are not your own; you were bought at a price. Therefore honor God with your body" (1 Corinthians 6:19-20). What an awesome thought—we are temples in which God dwells. We should take care of our bodies by eating properly, exercising regularly, and resting sufficiently, as our Lord has commanded. The apostle Paul wrote, "I buffet my body and make it my slave" (1 Corinthians 9:27, NASB, 1973 edition). Some people joke that that he "buffeted" his body at the local smorgasbord. Not so.

Physical pride says, "Look at me—I look better than you!" Most of us are careful not to let those thoughts slip out of our mouths (we are too humble for that), but we do carry those attitudes around with us. In 1 Timothy 2:9-10 Paul writes, "I also want women to dress modestly, with decency and propriety, not with braided hair or gold or pearls or expensive clothes, but with good deeds, appropriate for women who profess to worship God." This passage, applicable not only to women but to all of us, is not saying that we are not permitted to better ourselves or to look sharp. Paul is speaking about prayer and worship and our attitudes when we come together to exalt His name. It is easy for any of us to spend more time thinking about what we're going to wear to church than in preparing to worship. Attitude and motive are key.

Some people say we should wear our best for God. Well, I think God is more interested in what's in my heart while sitting in church than what label I'm wearing. Can you imagine telling God, "Lord, I wore this Ralph Lauren polo shirt that cost $75 for You"? Or "Lord, I just came to praise Your name in my Liz Claiborne suit because You deserve my best"? Jesus quoted Isaiah when he warned the Pharisees, who put so much emphasis on the externals, "These people honor me with their lips, but their hearts are far from me. They worship me in vain; their teachings are but rules taught by men" (Matthew 15:8, quoting Isaiah 29:13). Such a sin is so subtle, but when we spend too much time fixing ourselves up for church or any other public event, secretly wanting people to notice us, we are falling short of God's will. We are not as concerned about their seeing the Spirit of Christ in us as we are about their noticing how well we look. That's pride.

In America we have turned the human body into an idol to worship. We love the created more than the Creator. The movie industry is all about finding the best-looking people and then putting them on display in such a way that viewers worship them. Pornography is another form of worship. It not only reduces women to being mere objects, which is wrong in itself, it not only encourages and enables sexual lust, but it also turns its users into worshipers of human anatomy. This sin goes deeper than lust or uncontrolled passion. It is idolatry.

We must reject the idea that image is everything and come back to what is important to God. He wants us to trust in Him, not in our appearance or our fashion or others' misplaced admiration.

SPIRITUAL PRIDE

Jesus gave His disciples a perfect example of spiritual pride when he told them the story of the Pharisee and the tax collector in Luke 18.

> *To some who were confident of their own righteousness and looked down on everybody else, Jesus told this parable: "Two men went up to the temple to pray, one a Pharisee and the other a tax collector. The Pharisee stood up and prayed about himself: 'God, I thank you that I am not like other men—robbers, evildoers, adulterers—or even like this tax collector. I fast twice a week and give a tenth of all I get.' But the tax collector stood at a distance. He would not even look up to heaven, but beat his breast and said, 'God, have mercy on me, a sinner.' I tell you that this man, rather than the other, went home justified before God. For everyone who exalts himself will be humbled, and he who humbles himself will be exalted."*
>
> —VERSES 9-14

We have all played the role of the Pharisee at various times in our spiritual journey and have had the attitude that we're not quite as bad as other people we know. In fact, there are some in our churches today who feel that God is lucky to have them in His family. In their minds they never really sin, and even if they do, it certainly is not serious enough to earn God's disfavor.

In this story Jesus reveals the depravity of the human heart and brings to light our wrong motives. We know from Luke 18 that some people came to Jesus confident of their spirituality. They knew they were better than the rest, and they were proud of that "fact." There is no room for God when we feel we are perfect and in need of nothing. We don't trust Him because we trust our own goodness. Jesus then gave this incredible example of the kind of heart He's looking for in His children. The Pharisee makes the mistake of classifying sins as serious or non-serious. He mentions the ones to the Lord that he felt made a person a real sinner. To that self-righteous Pharisee, the sins of robbers, evildoers, adulterers, and tax collectors were the worst. Blinded by the log in his own eyes, he couldn't see the sins in his life that were alienating him from God. Thomas à Kempis wrote, "Gladly we desire to make other men perfect, but we will not amend our own faults." The Pharisees were always pointing out the faults of others, yet failing to see or admit their own sinful arrogance.

I often reflect on the numerous times I have played the role of the Pharisee, when I have been quick to judge a brother for his sin while conveniently overlooking my own sin. We tend to be proud of the sins we don't commit but ignore the ones staring us in the face. It's like the person who is always speaking against the addiction of drugs and alcohol, yet is guilty of gluttony. How can I preach to others about the sin of lust when I hold on to the sin of gossip? We have the strange notion that somehow our own sins are not as vile as those of others. As we sit in church services and hear messages that bring to light certain transgressions that might be separating us from God's blessings in our lives, we look around the congregation to identify those whom the minister is targeting. And of course it's not us! It is always the other person.

Once we have taken on the attitude of the Pharisees, thinking our sins are minuscule or nonexistent, we run the risk of believing that God would not dare judge us for our trivial sins.

To use a modern expression, we feel we are "above the law." King Saul believed he was above the law, but he had a rude awakening.

The people of Israel had been complaining that they wanted a king like other nations. Isn't it peculiar how we seem to want to copy the world? In 1 Samuel we find the story of how God took a humble man, Saul, and exalted him to the position of king. Saul was not seeking the position; in fact, when they came to anoint him king he was hiding in some baggage. Once Saul was confirmed as king, at first he led the people to follow the Lord as Samuel the prophet had instructed him to do. But then spiritual pride set in.

On numerous occasions the Lord was displeased with Saul because he failed to completely fulfill His commands. Saul, like many of us, would change the instructions just a little so it would meet a need in his life. He would obey the Lord, but not completely. There was always some little area that was not right, and Saul always justified himself in what he had done. His words sounded spiritual, but they were only a smoke screen for his own greed and selfishness.

The end of Saul's reign came with the battle against the Amalekites. In 1 Samuel 15, the Lord gave clear and specific instructions through the prophet Samuel. "Samuel said to Saul, 'I am the one the LORD sent to anoint you king over his people Israel; so listen now to the message from the LORD. This is what the LORD Almighty says: "I will punish the Amalekites for what they did to Israel when they waylaid them as they came up from Egypt. Now go, attack the Amalekites and totally destroy everything that belongs to them. Do not spare them; put to death men and women, children and infants, cattle and sheep, camels and donkeys."'"

Saul prepared for the battle by assembling 200,000 soldiers to go up against them. That must have been an impressive sight. "Then Saul attacked the Amalekites all the way from Havilah to Shur, to the east of Egypt. He took Agag king of the Amalekites alive, and all his people he totally destroyed with the sword. But Saul and the army spared Agag and the best of the sheep and cattle, the fat calves and lambs—everything that was good. These they were unwilling to destroy completely, but everything that was despised they totally destroyed."

Do you see the mind-set here? Saul only partially obeyed the Lord, which means that in reality he disobeyed the Lord. Saul thought to himself, *Certainly the Lord won't mind; after all, I'm the king, and I should receive some of the spoils of war.* Saul made a huge mistake—one that was irreversible.

The battle was over, and the celebrations had begun. Saul was living the good life, especially since he had just added some new investments to his personal portfolio, so to speak. Saul had no idea that far away the Lord was giving instruction to Samuel the prophet regarding the decommissioning of King Saul. With the instruction clear, Samuel went to visit the celebrating king.

> *When Samuel reached him, Saul said, "The LORD bless you! I have carried out the LORD's instructions." But Samuel said, "What then is this bleating of sheep in my ears? What is this lowing of cattle that I hear?" Saul answered, "The soldiers brought them from the Amalekites; they spared the best of the sheep and cattle to sacrifice to the LORD your God, but we totally destroyed the rest." "Stop!" Samuel said to Saul. "Let me tell you what the LORD said to me last night." "Tell me," Saul replied. Samuel said, "Although you were once small in your own eyes, did you not become the head of the tribes of Israel? The LORD anointed you king over Israel. And he sent you on a mission, saying, 'Go and completely destroy those wicked people, the Amalekites; make war on them until you have wiped them out.' Why did you not obey the LORD? Why did you pounce on the plunder and do evil in the eyes of the LORD?"*
>
> 1 SAMUEL 15:13-19

Saul in his spiritual pride thought he was above the law. When confronted, he could only blame others, make excuses, and tell lies regarding his noble motivation to use the forbidden items as a sacrifice to the Lord. As a result of Saul's phony confession, we hear the Lord saying through Samuel, "To obey is better than sacrifice" (verse 22).

Saul had started off being a man of humility, yet in the end he became a man full of pride, believing that what God said could be amended to fit his own desires. God's rules applied to others, not himself. Proverbs 27:21 says, "The crucible for silver and the furnace for gold, but man is tested by the praise he receives."

There are Christians today who believe they are above God's laws and that they can live any way they want and God won't touch them. There are ministers and so-called Christian leaders who feel they are above the law because of their service for God. A minister once said to me that he felt many leaders were getting caught in sin that they thought God would excuse because they were so important to His kingdom. Those of us in the ministry should never forget that we can be replaced. Saul lost his position due to his sin and his pride. We can lose our positions and our influence through the sin of spiritual pride. You may have a love for money or things it will buy. You may secretly be indulging in pornography. You may be living for the praise of others. You may be abusing your calling and be manipulating your congregation. Remember, you are not above God's law, and He will take steps to remove you if you don't change. Are we living our lives His way or ours?

Chapter 5

CONFESSIONS OF A CONTROL FREAK

I hate flying on airplanes! I have always hated flying, and I will always hate flying. Although I fly more than 100,000 miles a year, I never enjoy it. When the tires finally touch the ground, it's time to *celebrate*.

It has always been amazing to me that the airline industry intentionally uses words and phrases that tend to make people feel uncomfortable. *Terminal*, *departure*, *emergency exits*, and *oxygen mask* remind you that your days on earth are limited. And there's more. When you check in, airline personnel ask questions intended to thwart a terrorist who gets his kicks out of blowing up planes. To make matters even more unsettling, when you fly overseas you're asked to fill out a slip of paper with the phone number of your next of kin just in case the plane doesn't make it to its "final destination"! Now I'm ready to go jump on a plane. Right!

As I have sat for endless hours on planes, I have contemplated why I hate to fly. Is it the near misses, the clear-air turbulence, or the fact that the plane is loaded with 90,000 pounds of fuel (flammable of course)? What is it that makes me feel so uncomfortable as we rumble down the runway?

The issue is very simply CONTROL! Once I step on that plane, I have given up control of my life to the two people in the cockpit. Even though the flight attendants are always so cheerful when they announce who's in control of the plane, it doesn't make me feel any better. I've never met the captain and first officer, and I don't know a thing about them and what they were doing the night before. In my mind they are all suspect, and I don't like giving control of my life to someone I don't know.

In all my years of flying I've never had a captain come back and ask me my opinion on what course of action we should take. Rather, I'm told to sit in my seat and enjoy the flight at 36,000 feet in the air while traveling at 550 miles per hour in an aluminum gas can with wings. I have no control of my situation. When I'm in my car I am able to make my own decisions and judgments, but when flying I am totally in the hands of the people on the flight deck. They are in control, and I am not.

I've met many people who have that same desire for control. I've met others, and you have as well, who not only like to control their own lives but also the lives of others—sometimes their spouses, sometimes their children, even though their sons or daughters are grown and married. Others feel the need to control the church and the decision-making process in that body. Other people always control the conversation, directing it to places that are safe or self-serving. Yes, for many of us control is the thing we most desire in life, and we're frustrated and angry when we don't have it.

It's funny that many people who feel compelled to be in charge or control don't think of themselves in that light at all. They usually see themselves as helpful, only wanting the best for somebody else. In their view, they sacrifice for the good of others and do more than their fair share of the work. They often have no idea that they drive people crazy and, in the worst cases, actually drive people away, including the people they love.

I've met people who are horrified to find out that others think they're a real pain in the neck because they always have to have their own way. They have no idea that people actually despise them for their inflexibility and their inability to compromise for a common goal. I have spoken to husbands and dads who were brokenhearted to realize that the family they protect and provide for actually finds them to be tyrannical. I have counseled church members who were shocked to find out that people see them in a very negative light. They couldn't understand how they could be so misunderstood. Meanwhile, those around them could not understand how they could be so pushy, demanding, and aggressive.

I must confess that I have been on both sides of the fence. I have seen the incredible controlling nature of people in the churches I've served, and I have been confronted by my own family regarding my lack of flexibility. What I considered as being a good, caring, practical father was perceived as being controlling, inflexible, and no fun at all. That was hard to come to grips with. I had a picture of the person I thought I was, but those who were closest to me had a completely different picture. At first I brushed their complaints aside and comforted myself in the thoughts that they had no idea how demanding it was to be the leader, provider, and protector. But I have learned over and over in life that what is perceived is indeed a reality to those who perceive it, and it must be dealt with in such a way.

So it was back to the spiritual drawing board. As I spent time with the Lord, I began to see that my need to control my family was motivated by fear and a lack of trust in God. I was saying to God that I had to control everything in the Owens family because He was not capable of running day-to-day operations. When I am in control, God is not. When I make all the decisions, God does not. When I have to be the provider, God cannot. I realized I had sinned against God once more by forgetting that my wife and children are His children and that He will take care of His children! If you are a father, you know the struggle we face in giving our families to the Lord. Something deep within us drives us to protect our families at all costs. I cannot imagine the horror of those in war-torn lands who have seen their children and wives tortured, raped, and killed in front of their very eyes. And this desire to protect is God-given. But out of balance with our own trust in the Lord, it becomes domination rather than leadership.

All the while we are striving to keep control of our lives, our families, and our situations, God is desiring for us to yield it all to Him. Men need predictability, perhaps more than women. We like life to be like a sheet of graph paper, with clear lines showing precise directions and delineations. When the lines aren't clear, for whatever reason, we begin to feel out of control and we struggle for balance. I have met men who came to the Lord as a result of this very real struggle. God brought them to a place where they could no longer control their lives. God is creative in how he brings us to this point of trusting Him.

At an evangelistic crusade in the Midwest, I spoke to the community's civic leaders at a luncheon. I asked those present, "Is this all there is to life? We live, we marry, we work, we have children, we retire, and we die?" I then went on to give a clear presentation of the Gospel, and at the end of my message I invited those present to put their faith in Jesus Christ. One man who trusted Christ was forty-three and dying of cancer. He told me he knew he was no longer in control and was afraid. At the point of utter despair, he cried out to God in faith and repentance.

God is always moving in our lives in order to grow our faith in Him. Faith is born out of our experiences with God. The Word of God is filled with narratives of people just like you and me whose faith grew as they saw the mighty works of God in their lives. They experienced God for themselves, and their faith was strengthened, and yet they continued to struggle with completely trusting God.

One such man was Gideon, a man I can relate to, because he was hesitant to relinquish control of his life and circumstances to God. Three chapters in the book of Judges chronicle the development of Gideon's faith and the work that God did through him. God led him one step at a time, like a father with a small child, giving him time to experience God and to grow in faith.

The time was around 1100 B.C., and the Israelites were settled in the land that the Lord had promised to them through Abraham. Once again they had yielded to the temptation of their day and turned their hearts to false gods. It appears that the Lord used the Midianites to manifest His displeasure with their idolatry, and they paid dearly for it.

> *Again the Israelites did evil in the eyes of the* LORD, *and for seven years he gave them into the hands of the Midianites. Because the power of Midian was so oppressive, the Israelites prepared shelters for themselves in mountain clefts, caves and strongholds. Whenever the Israelites planted their crops, the Midianites, Amalekites and other eastern peoples invaded the country. They camped on the land and ruined the crops all the way to Gaza and did not spare a living thing for Israel, neither sheep nor cattle nor donkeys. They came up with their livestock and their tents like swarms of locusts. It was impossible to count the men and their camels; they invaded the land to ravage it. Midian so impoverished the Israelites that they cried out to the* LORD *for help.*
>
> JUDGES 6:1-6

After the hours of news footage we have seen from places like Bosnia and Kosovo, we can easily picture what was happening to the children of Israel. This was an especially fearful time. For one thing, no other country had used camels in warfare against Israel, giving the Midianites greater mobility. Life for Israel was chaotic, with no certainty of safety or sustenance day by day. This is where the farm boy Gideon comes on the scene.

Gideon was out doing his daily chores of threshing wheat when the angel of the Lord appeared before him and said, "The LORD is with you, mighty warrior." Taken aback, Gideon stated the obvious to the angel: "If the LORD is with us, why has all this happened to us?" (verses 12-13).

The angel continued his announcement to Gideon by telling him he was the one who would lead Israel to victory over these troublesome Midianites. "The LORD turned to him and said, 'Go in the strength you have and save Israel out of Midian's hand. Am I not sending you?'"

Gideon's response was one of either humility, fear, or a little of both. "But LORD, how can I save Israel? My clan is the weakest in Manasseh, and I am the least in my family." But the Lord quickly let Gideon know that he would have success because of the power of God, not because of himself.

Gideon was starting to see the ramifications of this conversation. He was just a man with a farm tool in his hand, and he has just been given the military position of general. Since the Midianite army was about 135,000 strong, this was going to be a serious battle, not a minor skirmish. Because of the circumstances and because of his own background, I'm sure he had self-doubt regarding his ability to lead others into battle. We men want to appear competent at all times. If something threatens that, we either respond with more aggressive behavior or we bail out completely. Most men do not like to learn to do something new, especially when other men are watching. Some of my most uncomfortable moments have been trying to hit a golf ball in front of others who were very good at it. As silly as it seems, I felt inferior. I have been on the other side when trying to teach men how to hit a tennis ball. I can see the humiliation in their posture as the ball continues to sail off the court. We want to appear competent at all times, in work or play, and I am sure Gideon was no different.

Deciding he'd better get control of the situation before he embarrassed himself, he asked the angel to wait for a minute while he went to get some things to test this messenger from the Lord. The angel of the Lord obliged Gideon, who came back with a cooked goat and some bread and set it before his guest. Some have thought Gideon acted shrewdly. If his guest ate the food, he would be a mere man, at best a prophet. But if the guest viewed the food as an offering, then Gideon would see the power of God. To Gideon's delight, the angel gave him specific instructions. "Take the meat and the unleavened bread, place them on this rock, and pour out the broth." Once Gideon obeyed, the Lord was ready to reveal Himself. "With the tip of the staff that was in his hand, the angel of the LORD touched the meat and the unleavened bread. Fire flared from the rock, consuming the meat and the bread. And the angel of the LORD disappeared. When Gideon realized that it was the angel of the LORD, he exclaimed, 'Ah, Sovereign LORD! I have seen the angel of the LORD face to face!'"

Gideon was feeling better now. The Lord was with him. But before the Lord would give him the big assignment of saving the nation, He gave him the smaller assignment of saving his own home. Scripture is clear that Gideon's father worshiped the pagan god Baal. God told Gideon to tear down his father's altar to the pagan god and build a proper one to the Lord in its place. Gideon knew this would cause quite a row in his family as well as with the neighbors.

Gideon obeyed the Lord, though, to keep a degree of control over the situation, he completed his assignment at night "because he was afraid of his family and the men of the town" (6:27). I understand why Gideon acted under cover of darkness, coming up with a plan of his own instead of totally trusting in the Lord's protection. I have done this myself many times. Obedient to the Lord? Yes. Well, almost. I want to still have some measure of control. If the Lord lets me down or doesn't do it the way I think He should, I have *my* systems in place to finish the job. As someone once said to me, "I trust God for the things I know I can accomplish myself." Sad, but true of all of us.

Once Gideon's actions were known, there was an outcry to have him killed. Thankfully his father rose to the occasion and in uncharacteristic fashion put Baal to the test. If Baal wanted his son to die, he said, Baal could do it himself. This argument seemed to satisfy the mob, and Gideon's faith grew a bit more as he saw that the Lord was true to His word.

For those of us who like to stay in control of situations, Gideon's next challenge of faith sends chills down our spines. Gideon now accepted the fact that he was going to lead the army in battle against the dreaded Midianites; so he called for the assembling of the army. But still wanting some control of the situation—perhaps even some control of God—Gideon decided it was fleece time! "If you will save Israel by my hand as you have promised—look, I will place a wool fleece on the threshing floor. If there is dew only on the fleece and all the ground is dry, then I will know that you will save Israel by my hand, as you said" (6:36-37). The next morning Gideon found the fleece saturated with water, so much so that he squeezed out a full bowl. He also found the ground to be very dry.

Perhaps Gideon thought, *Maybe that was just a coincidence*. Have you ever thought that about something you'd prayed for? Maybe you laid out a fleece before the Lord and He answered you, but you still doubted Him. Gideon asked the Lord to do it one more time—only in reverse. How creative!

"Do not be angry with me," he said to the Lord. "Let me make just one more request. Allow me one more test with the fleece. This time make the fleece dry and the ground covered with dew." God granted him his request, and now Gideon was satisfied that the Lord was going to deliver the Midianites into his hands.

I'm fairly proud of Gideon for asking God to do the fleece thing only twice. There have been times in my life when my faith was so small and my desire to control so great that I asked for more fleeces than two!

Now Gideon stood before his army of 32,000 men, knowing that against 135,000 Midianites they had difficult work before them. But with 32,000 men and with Gideon in charge . . . But as the story unfolded, the Lord made it clear that He didn't want Gideon in control of the battle at all. God wanted Gideon and those fighting alongside him to put their trust in God, and in God only. That's the same lesson the Lord is continually trying to teach us. "Trust Me! Trust Me!"

> *The* LORD *said to Gideon, "You have too many men for me to deliver Midian into their hands. In order that Israel may not boast against me that her own strength has saved her, announce now to the people, 'Anyone who trembles with fear may turn back and leave Mount Gilead.'" So twenty-two thousand men left, while ten thousand remained.*
>
> 7:2-3

This is where the control freak would lose it. The odds now stand at 13 to 1 in the Midianites' favor! I can just imagine Gideon trying to pump himself up for this battle with only 10,000 men. "We can do this. We're bad. We can take 'em." But God wanted absolute control for *His* glory, not for Gideon's. So, "the Lord said to Gideon, 'There are still too many men.'"

Gideon must've thought, *You've got to be kidding me! Too many men? Is the Lord seeing the same thing I'm seeing? They have 135,000 men and I have 10,000. What channel is He watching?* Then the Lord said, "Take them down to the water, and I will sift them for you there. If I say, 'This one shall go with you,' he shall go; but if I say, 'This one shall not go with you,' he shall not go."

Gideon is not feeling so competent right now. Not only has the Lord decommissioned two-thirds of his army, but the Lord has taken over the final selection process. Gideon has no say in the matter. He can only trust and obey!

> *So Gideon took the men down to the water. There the* LORD *told him, "Separate those who lap the water with their tongues like a dog from those who kneel down to drink." Three hundred men lapped with their hands to their mouths. All the rest got down on their knees to drink. The* LORD *said to Gideon, "With the three hundred men that lapped I will save you and give the Midianites into your hands. Let all the other men go, each to his own place." So Gideon sent the rest of the Israelites to their tents but kept three hundred, who took over the provisions and trumpets of the others.*
>
> VERSES 5-8

If my math is correct, this makes it about 450 to 1—a mark of insanity and sure suicide in the world's eyes.

In order for our faith in God to grow, He brings us to the place where we are convinced that only God could've brought the victory. As long as we try to control people, circumstances, and our environment, we will never experience God by seeing the miraculous in our lives. F. B. Meyer, the late British preacher and writer, said it best: "You never test the resources of God until you attempt the impossible."

Once Gideon yielded and decided that he should and would take the Lord at His word, he saw the incredible resources of God. God used those 300 men to defeat the huge Midianite army and chase them out of their land. God armed them with pots, trumpets, and torches—not exactly the usual weapons of choice for a war. They divided into three groups of 100 and stationed themselves on the sides of the Midianite camp. They were instructed to follow Gideon's lead of breaking the pot, blowing the trumpet, and holding the torch high. As all 300 men began to break their pots, they cried out in a loud voice, "A sword for the LORD and for Gideon!" The Lord used this seemingly silly plan to create such confusion in the camp that the Midianites began to kill each other; in fact, some were so frightened that they took their own lives. The Israelites captured the leaders of the Midianites and put them to death, thus ushering in a blessed time of freedom and peace. Gideon and the entire nation of Israel knew that this victory was the result of God's supernatural work. There was no other explanation.

Have you had supernatural experiences in your life? Can you recall times when only the Lord could have done a certain thing and your faith grew deeper as a result? As long as I think I have to appear competent and hold onto the steering wheel of my life, I miss seeing the mighty hand of God at work.

I have discovered several reasons for fighting for control in my life. One is pride that makes me think *my* way is best. This often comes out in my marriage and family relationships.

Fear of the unexpected is another reason. I am afraid of how I will react in a new situation. I don't want to be uncomfortable; I want to be, and especially to appear, competent.

I also fight for control because it meets a need in my life. I want to feel important and needed. Sometimes we create crises so we can fix them and in turn feel better about ourselves. I see this happen a lot in church board meetings. The controlling person often has an extraordinary sense of worthlessness.

I may also feel the need to control when I am dealing with anger in my heart. Angry people need to control. Unfortunately, that need to control is usually directed at other people—people they love.

In his book *Don't Sweat the Small Stuff*, Dr. Richard Carlson writes a chapter for those who always have to be right. Have you been there? So have I. Dr. Carlson writes:

> Being right, defending our positions, takes an enormous amount of mental energy and often alienates us from the people in our lives. Many people, consciously or unconsciously, believe that it's somehow their job to show others how their positions, statements, and point of view are incorrect, and that in doing so, the person they are correcting is going to somehow appreciate it, or at least learn something. Wrong! (New York: Hyperion, 1997, page 33)

You might ask, "How do I know if I am overcontrolling?" Actually, that is usually fairly easy to figure out, if we're willing to hear it. What are your family members telling you? What are your friends saying to you? Keep a journal for one day of your life, and see how many times you feel the need to control your life, the lives of others, to be right. Opening our eyes and seeing ourselves as others see us can be a startling revelation. I know it was for me. Ask the Lord to give you the wisdom to see yourself as you really are and to release the controls to Him. Why should you or I control other people when that is the Lord's responsibility? I sometimes still have to confess my sin of unbelief to the Lord when I realize I'm trying to wrestle back control and power over my life.

Four years ago I received a phone call at work from my wife. She said those dreaded words, "Dan, I think you'd better come home." As I walked through the door, I saw my wife sitting on the couch with tears flowing down her cheeks, and she informed me she was pregnant.

I'm sure you were thinking something more horrible was about to be announced. Well, when you're forty years old, you have two teenage sons, you're enjoying your wife's companionship when you travel, and your financial goals are in place, hearing that your wife is going to have a baby is a bit shocking. I sat and cried with her as we contemplated starting all over again with another child.

I'm ashamed to admit that I became angry and then depressed. This wasn't in my plans! This shouldn't have happened! My comfortable life was being messed up! I struggled with this for several months as I searched for space in our home for a new baby.

Not long afterward, while standing in the aisle of an airplane that had just landed, I looked behind me and saw a mother with a baby. I made the negative comment that with two teenagers in my home I was about to have an "oops" baby enter our lives. A man standing next to me looked at me with pain in his eyes. "You are so lucky!" he said. "My wife and I have been trying to have a baby for years."

That's all it took for the Lord to bring me back to my senses and reveal that the reason I was so upset with being a father again was my need to control. Back to my knees I went.

Now Taylor is three years old, and I cannot imagine life without him (but I am not planning on child number four either, though that's in God's hands). "Let go and let God"—God has had to remind me of that too many times. But maybe that's what you need to do today. Let go of the controls and let God be God. He is much more capable than we are—always.

Chapter 6

I DON'T BELIEVE

Bodega Bay in Northern California is famous for being the location for Alfred Hitchcock's movie *The Birds*, but for me it's a place of adventure. I first dived for abalone off the rocks lining the shore there and discovered the beautiful world under the vast Pacific Ocean. It was also at Bodega Bay that I had my first experience on a charter fishing boat. I was seventeen. What a thrill to jump on board a boat that for once in my life was larger than a ski boat. The boat was complete with a captain and crew and all the stuff one needs for fishing the ocean depths, including food for us to ease the boredom of the long ride out to sea.

It took almost two hours to get to where the captain felt we should be in order to ensure that we would take home our limit of lingcod, rock cod, and sea bass, and who was going to argue with the captain. As we surfed over the gentle waves, many of the men helped themselves to the coffee and pastries included in the day's package. For me, I was happy to stand in the bow and let the wind and the saltwater spray buffet my body.

Just as we were beginning to feel a bit of restlessness, the big diesel engines died down, and the air became incredibly quiet.

An anchor was released to hold our position as the swells moved us around with ease. Now the fun began. Each man began to prepare his fishing gear with care and quiet pride. The bait was made available in big buckets, and it didn't take long for the first salvo of fishing lines to hit the water. Each man found his own place to sit with coffee and pole in hand to wait for the battle to come. I promptly baited my two hooks and let the weights pull my line over the edge of the boat and into the sea. I had never caught fish in the ocean before, and I certainly didn't want to be the last one on the boat to have that thrill.

I had never been this far out into the ocean before. In fact, I had never really ventured out past the bays of Northern California. Even in the exhilaration of the moment I was awed by the amount of water that surrounded us. The shoreline was barely visible.

Our seasoned captain had selected the right spot, and the fish began to take the bait. I hadn't been sitting too long before I felt a pull on my line, and I swiftly yanked on my pole to set the hook. Reeling this first fish in was much harder than I expected. I had forgotten how far down my hooks were and how heavy the sinkers were even without a fish. After many minutes of pulling up my pole, creating slack, and reeling the slack in rapidly, the muscles in my arms were beginning to burn. Just when I thought I might be embarrassed by having to ask for help, the first fish broke the water! It was a large rock cod, fighting to stay in its domain under the sea. Adrenaline kicked in once I saw the fish, and I furiously fought to get it on board quickly. To my amazement, I had a fish on my second hook as well. I landed both fish and was quite proud of what I had just done. I was a deep-sea fisherman!

The boat was filled with laughter, fish stories, and lots of fish. We were having the time of our lives, and no one was in a hurry for the day to end. It seemed to come out of nowhere when the captain yelled, "Cut your lines now!" The gently rolling swells had become steep, wind-driven walls of water that were higher than the captain's housing on the top of the boat. The engines were called upon, and the anchor was put back in its place on board. To the protection of the bay we headed, our trip cut short by a storm we hadn't even seen coming.

The boat that seemed so large and sturdy now seemed uncomfortably small next to the waves that were pitching us this way and that at will. We alternated between being on the very crest of a wave to being in the trough with walls of water on both sides of the boat. Many of the men who had been laughing and eating pastries and other delicacies that their wives had packed for them were now vomiting over the side of the boat. One man who had been in the center of all the hoopla now sat huddled in a corner, his face as green as the Grinch.

The sky darkened, the rain shot from the clouds, and the waves grew bigger and bigger. The boat moved at a much slower pace as it fought against the elements, and our two hours coming out turned into about three and a half going in. We all sat there and wondered how much the boat could take and feared that one of those monstrous waves would swamp us. No one dared ask the captain how we were doing for fear that the news would not be good.

Seeing the mouth of Bodega Bay brought an incredible sense of relief. We were soaked, cold, and, let's be honest, terrified! The mood changed back to the levity of the early morning once we were in the safety of the bay. Every man knew this was going to be a story told again and again through the years. My first experience on the ocean was an unforgettable one.

The Gospel of Mark tells the story of a storm I can relate to very well. We find the story unfolding in Mark 4:35-41:

> *That day when evening came, he said to his disciples, "Let us go over to the other side." Leaving the crowd behind, they took him along, just as he was, in the boat. There*

> *were also other boats with him. A furious squall came up, and the waves broke over the boat, and it was nearly swamped. Jesus was in the stern, sleeping on a cushion. The disciples woke him and said to him, "Teacher, don't you even care if we drown?" He got up, rebuked the wind and said to the waves, "Quiet! Be still!" Then the wind died down and it was completely calm. He said to his disciples, "Why are you so afraid? Do you still have no faith?" They were terrified and asked each other, "Who is this? Even the wind and the waves obey him!"*

This story of Jesus and His disciples is not unlike my own. Their day was much like mine, with all the joy and expectations of a great day out on the water. Jesus had said to His disciples, "Let us go over to the other side." Can you picture the disciples telling Jesus not to worry about a thing, that they would take care of getting Him across? In so many words, I think the disciples said, "Go take it easy and leave the driving to us!" They were eager to show Jesus they knew a thing or two about sailing. The sun was shining, the provisions were loaded, and the disciples, who at one time made their living on the water, were feeling at home and loving it.

The Sea of Galilee brings to mind gentle sea breezes, blue water, sunny skies, and families at play. A picture of serenity. However, like America's Great Lakes, that sea can give birth to furious storms. Gordon Lightfoot's song "The Wreck of the Edmund Fitzgerald" describes in detail the events leading up to the sinking of a massive ship on Lake Superior. The Sea of Galilee has been known to exhibit waves as high as twenty feet when storms appear, seemingly, out of nowhere.

Mark intimates that the events of the next several hours were not due to some irresponsibility on the part of the disciples or their lack of planning. The storm was a complete surprise. Men of the sea commanded the boat. Men who could read the winds and the waves. Men who had been in storms before. But this storm brought the fear of death. I can picture those black thunderclouds, the cold, biting winds, sheets of driving rain, and mountainous waves. And just imagine—this was happening at night ("when evening came"), when all was dark.

Their little boat was being tossed around, bobbing like a toy. Unlike my experience in the Pacific, the disciples were having problems with water in the boat, a sailor's worst nightmare. The small boat would go down into the trough, but before it could get back on top of the swell, the wave would break into the boat. Mark says it was "nearly swamped." That phrase means "filled to the full." It didn't look like they were going to make it. There was panic, fear, despair, horror, and hopelessness. This was an impossible situation, one that apparently was about to take their lives.

Then someone got an idea: "Maybe Jesus can help us out!" I'm sure there were skeptics on board. Sure, Jesus could turn water into wine and heal the sick, but what could He do with a storm like this? But gratefully someone thought of asking for His help.

We've all been hit with storms in life. They've come out of nowhere, taking us by surprise. A broken marriage, loss of a job, the death of a child, a debilitating disease. You may be going through a storm at this very moment and are doing everything you can to make it through, to make sense of it all. Here is where I see myself so clearly that it hurts. Did you notice how long it took the disciples to turn to Jesus? I'm sure they tried everything they knew to do in order to save themselves. Finally, when they ran out of ideas, they turned to Jesus. How many times have I done that very thing? The storm comes, I go into action, and in all the commotion I leave God out until the situation is so desperate that I can do nothing except call on Him.

But remembering the presence of Jesus was the beginning to the end of their problem. Once they turned to Jesus, a sense of peace swept over the situation.

When my son Jordan was a toddler, he and I were alone in the house one day as my wife was out with Ben. I was busy packing for a trip when I heard Jordan scream, "Dad!" I ran down the hallway wondering what terrible thing had happened to him. Jordan was sitting calmly in front of the television. With my heart still thumping, I asked what was wrong. "Oh nothing, Dad. I just wanted to make sure you were still here!" He wanted to feel secure. Have you ever felt that way with God? You just want to know that He's there with you and that He still cares.

Last night as I talked to a friend who called to tell me he was praying for my ministry, I was reminded that we don't always have the answers to the reason for our storms. But we can have the sense that God is with us. Although my friend is going through incredible physical and emotional pain, he was quick to say that he was also experiencing the abiding presence of God. It is during such storms that we sense the reality of God and are grateful for His fatherly heart.

During the storms that blast our lives, we are often filled with negative thoughts. We may think that God is out to get us or that He is angry with us because we're not living up to His standard. We forget that "God is love," that He cares for us very much, always. I know that my faith in God is a direct result of the intimacy we share together. The closer I am to Him, the more often I share my thoughts with Him, the more time I spend meditating on His Word, the more I will trust Him. Above all else in life, we must keep our relationship with Jesus current.

Do you ever borrow things from your neighbors? You run out of sugar and send the kids next door for some so you can finish making the cookies. Now, if you haven't spoken to your neighbors in months, or if you don't maintain a relationship with them, it feels a bit uncomfortable to borrow something from them. The relationship is not current. On the other hand, if you and your family interact with your neighbors throughout the week, and your kids play with their kids, you feel confident running over to their house for a cup of sugar. You have kept the relationship current.

When storms pummel our lives, much will depend on how current our relationship with Jesus is. Do I feel confident going to Him for comfort and direction, or do I feel estranged from Him because I have placed Him on my "inactive relationships" list? Our cars are outfitted with a spare tire that we take for granted, until we have a flat tire by the side of the road. The spare tire is for an emergency only. How often we treat the Lord like a spare tire. We use Him in an emergency, and when the emergency is over, our need for the Lord is over! We live our lives as we please until things don't go as planned, and then we cry out for help. On many occasions we feel embarrassed to seek the Lord because we know it has been a long time since we have enjoyed His presence. We know that we have only "used" the Lord and have not worshiped Him.

Many years ago I played football at Liberty University. I remember the first day of practice in the summer heat and humidity of Virginia. The coach gathered us around and held a football high in the air. "Gentleman," he said, "this is a football." He started that practice and every practice with the basics. Every day the team drilled on blocking and tackling. Wherever we are in our walk with the Lord, we must not forget to practice the basics. We may get tired of hearing about them and think, "Let's move on to something else"; but without the basics, we will not enjoy the presence of God, nor will we find it easy to put our trust in Him.

What are the basics?

STUDY GOD'S WORD

We find time for the things we really want to do. Have you ever noticed how hard it is to read the Bible, but how easy it is to read a hundred pages of a best-selling novel? I always have time to read the newspaper or my favorite magazine, yet I find it hard to squeeze out fifteen minutes to read the Bible, God's love letter to us.

All of us can feed ourselves with the Word of God. As I travel and preach in churches, I often hear people criticize their pastor. One complaint that does not sit well with me is when people say, "My pastor's messages just don't feed me!" That is more of an indictment of the parishioner than of the pastor. When my oldest sons were small, we fed them because they couldn't get the spoon to their mouths. In fact, the spoon would go everywhere but their mouths. Now that they are teenagers (except Taylor the toddler), they can feed themselves. It would look strange if while sitting in McDonald's I held the hamburger up to their mouths for them to take a bite. They are old enough to feed themselves!

Most Christians are old enough to feed themselves spiritually. If we can read, we can feed! We all have the same Bible, access to study materials, and, most important, the Holy Spirit to enlighten us! If you are depending only on your pastor to feed you once a week, you are going to be a weak Christian.

SPEND TIME IN PRAYER

This sounds easy, but it can actually be the hardest spiritual discipline. The Bible says we are to "pray continually" (1 Thessalonians 5:17), yet many of us barely begin. Why is it that if someone calls on us to pray at church, we can do so with great vigor, but when we are alone we can barely get the words out of our mouths or minds? Could it be that like the Pharisees we often pray in public as a self-centered act? It seems so much harder to pray when we are alone. No audience, no introductions, no stage, no microphone, just God and us!

I often tell new Christians that talking to God is like talking to your best friend, only with much more reverence. You and I can and should talk to God at any time. However, some people even have a hard time talking to friends. Many people are introverts by nature. They are not outgoing and social, and so even talking to God can be somewhat painful. I have found that writing to God is a helpful exercise. I have always told my sons that if they are having a problem and can't get the words out, they can write me a letter. So why not write letters to our heavenly Father?

Sometimes it's hard to communicate because we're afraid our emotions are going to get in the way. We're afraid that we're not going to clearly communicate what is in our hearts. I remember the first letter I received from Ben about a girl problem he had. I was thrilled to get the letter and then told him to go ask his mother—she understood girls better! I keep a prayer journal because sometimes I just cannot say what is really on my heart, so I write a letter to God. And God always reads them.

Spend time with God—let God speak to you through His Word; and speak to God in prayer. This is not a "feel good" exercise; this is the reality of knowing Jesus Christ. This is the truth that His Spirit bears witness with our spirit that we are His children. Keep your relationship with the Lord current so that when the storms come, you will think of the Lord first and run to Him. He is waiting for you!

I often wonder how people cope with tragedies in their lives when they do not turn to the Lord. In the narrative about Jesus calming the sea, Mark says there were other boats. What was it like for the people in those boats when the storm came up? Whom did they turn to when there was no Jesus in the back of the boat? Everyone suffers at one time or another. We all experience pain and suffering, whether it be physical, emotional, mental, or whatever. A missionary couple was horribly attacked, the husband beaten so badly that he almost died, and his wife and daughter taken into the jungle and raped. How can one overcome such emotional and physical trauma? How can one forgive those who do such horrible things? Only God's grace allows us to make it through storms of this severity. So whom do people who do not know Jesus go to for comfort and healing?

Newsweek magazine (January 2, 1992) said, "Today's teenager faces more adult-strength stresses than their predecessors did, and at a time when adults are much less available to help them." Regarding college and university students, *U. S. News and World Report* that same year said, "There is little doubt that the growing financial worries and parental expectations are behind much of the pressure-cooker atmosphere on the college campus today." The article went on to say that campus mental health professionals have seen a 30 to 50 percent increase in students seeking counseling for stress at major universities such as Harvard, as well as at local community colleges.

Think of the stress that a single mother deals with. Up early in the morning to get her children ready for another day. Pressure at work. Pressure to find child care. Feelings of guilt for not always being there for her children. Pressure to keep up a home and make the car payment. Exhaustion each night. Wondering if things will ever change!

I speak at a lot of men's conferences and am amazed at how stressed out most men are. At a library recently I found these titles on the covers of magazines for men:

> "Winning over Worry"
> "How to Stop Making Yourself Sick"
> "Stress First-Aid"
> "Facing Stress: Use it, Lose it, Live with It"

I'm sure that during the storm the disciples were in the most stressful situation of their lives. Their pride was gone; they had tried every trick they knew to save their boat and themselves. Things were so bad that they turned to a carpenter for help! They woke Jesus and said, "Teacher, don't you care if we drown?" They weren't asking politely either. They were upset with Jesus. There was anger in their tone of voice. "Don't You care? We've left everything to follow You. Our friends think we're crazy. Now You bring us out here in this storm and we're going to die!"

As a little boy I was afraid of going to school. I never felt comfortable being away from home and the nurturing nature of my mother. On most mornings during my elementary school years, I would wake up with a stomachache. I hated school and would do anything to stay home. Day after day, month after month, year after year my mom would come to my room to awaken me in the morning only to hear me beg her once again to let me stay home. The begging would turn to tears, a ritual that only a mother could endure. One morning my mom lost her patience and exploded. "Daniel, one of these days you are going to grow up and have a family of your own. I pray that you get a child just like you!"

It's funny how God sometimes answers the strangest prayer requests. As our first son entered kindergarten, I noticed that he was very uneasy about school. I also began to notice the same tricks that I'd used when I was a little boy, the tricks that would hopefully keep me home for the day. By the time he entered the first grade, he had a full-blown dislike of school just like his father used to have. The fake sicknesses along with the tears came each morning as he regretfully got ready for school. One morning as Deb and I were forcing him out the door to catch the bus, he turned and looked at me and said with tears coming down his little face, "Don't you even care?" My heart was broken. If anyone understood how he felt, I did. I assured Ben that I cared, but I also knew that he had to go to school and that everything would be all right. One of these days, I said, he would actually enjoy going to school and being with his friends. Fortunately, his dislike of school was very short-lived.

Have you ever wanted to ask God the same question Ben asked me that morning? "God, don't You even care?" When you feel alone and unloved, do you wonder where God is? When you feel like the stresses of life are about to sink you, do you wonder if God cares? When relationships deteriorate and there seems to be no way to recover them, do you ask God if He loves you anymore? Like the psalmist we ask, "How long will you hide your face from me?" (Psalm 13:1).

I watched my sister deal with her husband walking out on her never to return. I watched as she felt the blows of rejection and rode a roller coaster of emotions. I watched her bring her four children back home to live with my parents while she looked for a job. And I wondered, "God, don't You even care?" Life isn't always fair, and it certainly isn't easy. We may have times of peace and pleasure, but often our days are filled with disappointment and despair. Gone are the days when we pretended to live in perfect Christian homes with wonderful relationships abounding in every room. We know we are imperfect human beings who don't always see eye to eye with our spouse, and who don't always feel love coming from our children, and who don't always enjoy the life we've made for ourselves. Life can be hard and very unforgiving. I think the apostle Paul said it best in 2 Corinthians:

> *We are pressed on every side by troubles, but we are not crushed and broken. We are perplexed, but we don't give up and quit. We are hunted down, but God never abandons us. We get knocked down, but we get up again and keep going. Through suffering, these bodies of ours constantly share in the death of Jesus so that the life of Jesus may also be seen in our bodies.*
>
> 4:8-10, *New Living Translation*

Paul did not live in a fantasy world where everything was perfect. Where do we go as Christians when life begins to overwhelm us? We go to the promises of God. Jesus said to the disciples, "Let us go over to the other side." He didn't say, "Let's go get caught in a storm and drown." Jesus implicitly promised to get them to the other side of the lake. We must trust His promises.

What has God promised to us as we go through life on earth? Has He said life will be easy, that we will live problem-free? Some people believe that; some even preach it. If you've had the opportunity to meet people who have been tortured and imprisoned for Christ, you don't think that way. Millions of Christians today are being persecuted for their beliefs. Has God said that we will always be safe, that no harm will come to us? Columbine High School will always remind us that is not the case. Has God said we will never lose our jobs or be abandoned by a spouse? I meet Christians every week as I travel who tell me of failed marriages or terminal illness or some other deep tragedy. Jesus told His disciples they would experience tribulations. God doesn't promise us life without trials, but what does He offer us? What is His universal promise to us?

He has promised His continual presence: "Never will I leave you; never will I forsake you" (Hebrews 13:5). Those are not just nice words we quote when having a bad day. They communicate the reality of the Christian life: God is in us and with us and always will be. It is His presence that sustains those who are afflicted for their faith. Though imprisoned for years, separated from their families, they experience joy that goes beyond anything I have known. God gives grace to those who are going through the fire that is not experienced by those watching on the sidelines.

Even when we as believers in Jesus Christ feel alone, God is working on our behalf. He is changing us into the person He wants us to be for all eternity. I do not claim to understand how God thinks or works, but I do know that I am His son and He will do what is best for me and what is best for His eternal purposes. Although my body will eventually waste away, my spirit will be with Him in heaven forever and ever, according to His promise. We are just passing through this life on our way to a much better place, a place God has created for us.

As Jesus got up off his bunk and faced the storm, He was not at all alarmed. His peace was the same in the still waters and in the raging tempest. He was the creator of them both and could command the elements to respond to His will. Mark says, "He got up, rebuked the wind and said to the waves, 'Quiet! Be still!' Then the wind died down and was completely calm. He said to his disciples, 'Why are you so afraid? Do you still have no faith?'"

The disciples had seen Jesus perform miracles, but now they were the ones who needed a miracle! It is always easier to have faith for others and their circumstances than it is for my own. I have all the faith in the world if I'm praying for others and their problems. But when it comes to my own situations, I tend to worry and fret just like the disciples did. How comforting to know that they struggled in their faith even though they were in the actual physical presence of the Son of God! How good it is to be reminded that it is faith that pleases the Lord. God wants us to trust Him and Him alone! God is trying to build our faith little by little through our experiences of life.

Let the morning bring me word of your unfailing love,
for I have put my trust in you.
Show me the way I should go,
for to you I lift up my soul.
Rescue me from my enemies, O LORD,
for I hide myself in you.
Teach me to do your will,
for you are my God;
may your good Spirit
lead me on level ground.

PSALM 143:8-10

All of us need to experience the supernatural hand of God, to see solutions that do not originate with our own ingenuity but with God's love and power exercised on our behalf. We must see God at work! That is what builds our faith in Him. God leads us a step at a time, and faith builds more faith. We must see God at work in the small things so that as bigger events come our way we are able to trust Him then as well. Crossing the Sea of Galilee, the disciples were still little children of faith; but on the other side, as a result of their experience in the storm, their faith had grown a little stronger. They trusted Jesus a little more. "Who is this? Even the wind and the waves obey him!" He can calm the storms in our lives as well. We can trust Him and His promise to love us and watch over us.

Chapter 7

MICROWAVE VS. CROCK-POT

It was New Year's Day, and I was off to the store to find the missing ingredient Deb needed for one of her wonderful desserts. I took Ben and Jordan with me in hopes that we could divide and conquer in order to keep this shopping event as short as possible—after all, there were holiday parades and football games to be watched. On the way I asked the boys if they were going to make any New Year's resolutions. Ben was quick to fire back that he thought the whole idea was stupid. As a junior-higher, he'd already figured out that most resolutions were never kept anyway, so why even pretend. Oh, the wisdom of a fourteen-year-old.

Jordan, on the other hand, decided to turn the tables. "Dad, do you have a New Year's resolution?" I was proud to say that indeed I did. "What is it?" Before I could start a long discourse on what I felt I needed to work on for the year, Jordan took a guess. "Is it that you're going to be more patient this year?"

At that moment my New Year's resolution was changed. In his innocence Jordan had just told me what he thought was my greatest fault and therefore my greatest need. Patience. It didn't help that Ben was quick to laugh and agree with his little brother. I had come face to face with the reality that my sons saw me as a person who wasn't patient with them, life, or God. That was a blow to the fatherly image I had created for myself.

The lack of patience, or the sin of impatience if I want to be honest about it, was not only a character fault but also an indictment on my belief in God. The horrifying thing to me was that my ten-year-old son had already figured that out. I might say that I trust God, but my impatience with him says very much the opposite. A problem might arise, and I might say, "O Lord, I trust You," but I'm actually thinking, "I could fix this much faster! Look, Lord, if I just did this, moved that, changed this, it would all be taken care of." I might indeed trust the Lord, but I don't always trust His speed. Which really means once again that I am weak in my faith and I don't *really* trust Him.

Being impatient is something most of us can relate to. As someone has said, patience is something you admire in the driver behind you, but not in the one ahead of you. We all have areas where we can exercise "the patience of Job," and other places where we have no tolerance at all. You might have patience with people whose personality you can relate to, yet find yourself quickly irritable with others. You might have patience at home, but very little at your office. More likely, it's the other way around—impatience is magnified at home, as I learned from my sons.

The great pianist Ignacy Paderewski was asked by an admirer how he had become such an accomplished musician and composer. It must have taken a lot of patience to excel the way he had. "Everyone has patience," Paderewski remarked. "I learned to use mine." I'm guilty of not learning to use mine. Patience is hard work.

Our society is developing the most impatient generation yet. We live in an instant world where everything seems to be measured in seconds, or even nanoseconds. We want instant access to everything, and technology continues to make everything work quicker. Fast! Now! Instant! Immediate! That is how we live our lives. That is the American way.

A successful businessman and I were discussing the difference between baby boomers and their children. "They want everything right now," he said of the twenty-five-year-olds he employed. "Quick money and instant everything! They are the microwave generation where everything has to be *now*. I'm from the Crock-Pot generation where you let things take time and simmer."

Patience is a virtue of bygone days. In fact, in many segments of our society patience is considered a weakness of character and the absence of drive. In our day a person is praised for his hard-driving, aggressive, business-first behavior. It is certainly not uncommon for a man or woman to work sixty to seventy hours a week, week in and week out. An elder in our church made a point about his lack of available time to serve. He outlined his stress-filled week—not to complain, but to show the reality of life. He went on to say that he would easily log more than sixty hours that week and even more if his cell phone rang while he was on call. It's hard to be patient when moving at the speed of life in America!

Clearly the Bible teaches that the Lord very much wants to develop patience in us. In fact, patience is described as one of the characteristics of the Spirit-filled life in Galatians 522-23: "Love, joy, peace, patience . . ." Patience may not be popular, but it's godly. Jesus never seemed to be in a hurry. He knew the Father was in control, and He trusted Him. Do we trust our Father enough to wait on His timing and His leading? Do we really believe that He knows best? Can we be patient with God as He develops us to be the people He desires us to be?

Who doesn't like a shortcut? We love discovering shortcuts for everything from work to cooking. Modern appliances and conveniences were motivated by this desire. The only time I don't want a shortcut is when I'm riding my Harley because I want to stay on it as long as I can. I have come to realize that God seldom takes a shortcut, especially when it comes to the development of His children.

In Exodus 13 we read that Pharaoh finally gave up the fight against God and His people and allowed the Israelites to leave Egypt. But God didn't give them a shortcut to their destination. In fact, even though they wandered in the desert for an extra forty years, the Lord did not originally intend for them to take a shortcut to the Promised Land. "When Pharaoh let the people go, God did not lead them on the road through the Philistine country, though that was shorter. For God said, 'If they face war, they might change their minds and return to Egypt.' So God led the people around by the desert road toward the Red Sea" (verses 17-18). Read between the lines. Can you hear Moses presenting an alternate route? "Lord, if we go this way, it will be so much quicker. We can shave off a lot of time!" God knew they were not ready to face an enemy yet. They had been slaves for years. They were not an organized army ready for battle. God knew they needed time.

The Lord was not interested in the quickest route. He never is. God is always working on us and preparing us for the next step in His plan for our lives. The Israelites had to learn to wait on the Lord. They had to learn to yield and obey even when it didn't make sense to them. They had to trust God when He led them over a much slower route for their own protection. "Wait for the LORD; be strong and take heart and wait for the LORD" (Psalm 27:14). "We wait in hope for the LORD; he is our help and our shield. In him our hearts rejoice, for we trust in his holy name. May your unfailing love rest upon us, O LORD, even as we put our hope in you" (Psalm 33:20-22).

Some people are naturally more patient because of their temperament and personality. My wife has much more patience than I have; she has a much longer fuse than I do. Our temperaments are indeed different. But the fact that my personality is different from hers does not excuse me from practicing patience. Patience is a fruit of the Spirit that God wants to produce in each and every believer. Patience is not something you can work up; it is a quality the Lord, and only the Lord, builds into us. Like all the fruits of the Spirit, patience takes time to produce, and for some of us, it is a constant struggle to maintain it.

God seems to have a way of stretching our patience to its limits. I can only imagine Moses' frustration when he realized that the Lord was not going to allow him to lead the people on the shortest route between points A and B. Why the detour? It's easier for us to handle a no from God than it is to discover that He wants us to wait. The latter goes against our nature and our society. But God is not so much interested in our comfort as He is in our character. He is always working on us, conforming us to the image of His Son. Do I trust what He is doing in my life? Do I believe He is looking out for my best interests? Do I have faith that He is preparing me sufficiently and lovingly for the future?

In San Diego, where I live, both the Marines and the Navy have a strong presence. The Marine Training Center is right next to the airport. As planes take off, passengers can look down and see Marines in basic training. I'm always glad that it's them and not me climbing those ropes and going through the obstacle course. That training is not a vacation!

Glenn was proud that he had made it through basic training to become a Marine, and he explained why each new recruit has to endure so much discipline. Everything they do has a purpose. Nothing is by chance or accident. Glenn said when he first arrived at boot camp, he couldn't figure out why the drill instructor was so petty about little things. In the mess tent, for example, everyone had to hold his food tray a certain way while waiting in line—flat against his chest, right hand holding the top right corner, left hand holding the bottom left corner. What was the big deal? Why get yelled at and ordered to do push-ups for not holding the tray correctly? When Glenn was issued his M-

16, he understood. Shown how to hold the rifle while running or marching, Glenn was amazed that his hands were in the food-tray position. His hands had been trained three times a day to hold that rifle correctly.

We often don't understand why God does what He does in our lives. At times life just doesn't make sense. We have to remember that God is at work, and, as in the military, nothing is by chance or accident. To use an imperfect analogy, God is our drill instructor and is taking us through basic training so we can "be all that we can be" in Christ Jesus. God disciplines us for a reason!

God uses three forms of discipline to keep us from harm—corrective, preventative, and educational.

> *"My son, do not make light of the Lord's discipline, and do not lose heart when he rebukes you, because the Lord disciplines those he loves, and he punishes everyone he accepts as a son." Endure hardship as discipline; God is treating you as sons. For what son is not disciplined by his father? If you are not disciplined (and everyone undergoes discipline), then you are illegitimate children and not true sons. Moreover, we have all had human fathers who disciplined us and we respected them for it. How much more should we submit to the Father of our spirits and live! Our fathers disciplined us for a little while as they thought best; but God disciplines us for our good, that we may share in his holiness. No discipline seems pleasant at the time, but painful. Later on, however, it produces a harvest of righteousness and peace for those who have been trained by it.*
>
> HEBREWS 12:5-11

Should we be surprised by this passage of Scripture? Does it cause us to be offended? Consider the *corrective discipline* I have given my sons. When they were little and the ball would go into the street, they were *not* to chase it. "Dad will get it!" Did they always obey? No. I would see them chase the ball into the street, and on more than one occasion I would see a car slowing down, waiting for my sons to retrieve the ball. What would I do when I saw this happen? I would discipline them to correct their behavior. Did I do this because I did not love them? No. In fact, my motivation was very much the opposite. It was out of love that I spanked them. I didn't want them to get hurt. I would tell them, "I can replace the ball, but I can't replace you. If you get hit by a car, the car will win!"

God always disciplines out of love in order to correct behavior or attitudes that are harmful. When He corrected David after that king committed adultery and was an accomplice to murder, He did so out of His love for David. When God corrected the church at Corinth, He did so because of His love for the people of that church. When God corrects you, He does so because you are His child and He wants what's best for you. We should not "lose heart" but should instead be grateful when God corrects us, accepting His discipline as proof that we belong to Him.

God also uses *preventative discipline* in our lives, as parents do with their children. Why do we respond so strongly when we discover that one of our children has told a lie? What are we worried about? We all know of people who began to tell lies when they were young, and nobody stopped them. Lying became an easy thing to do and a normal part of their daily life. As they got older, they couldn't tell the truth from a lie, and their lives became one big deceitful story.

Someone has put this pattern in an especially clever way: "Sow an act and you reap a habit. Sow a habit and you reap a character. Sow a character and you reap a destiny." Many people's destinies have been less than good due to their lack of discipline. The Bible says we destroy our own children if we do not use preventative discipline in their lives.

The apostle Paul understood this principle very well. In 2 Corinthians, after he had shared in detail regarding a special encounter with God, he said that God helped him keep a lid on his pride.

> *To keep me from becoming conceited because of these surpassingly great revelations, there was given me a thorn in my flesh, a messenger of Satan, to torment me. Three times I pleaded with the Lord to take it away from me. But he said to me, "My grace is sufficient for you, for my power is made perfect in weakness."*
>
> 12:7-9

Paul had an understanding of God's preventative discipline. After receiving so many of God's extraordinary blessings, he could have been really puffed up, but God prevented him from becoming a sinfully proud person. There are times, however, when we do not understand why God appears to make things hard on us. We are not always sure what He is trying to prevent from happening in our lives. This is where we must exercise faith and believe that God is working for our good, choosing to walk by faith and not sight. God's motivation to use preventative discipline is the same as His motivation when he uses corrective discipline. *He loves us.* J. I. Packer has written, "Your heavenly Father loves you enough to school you in holy living. Appreciate what he is doing and be ready for the rough stuff that his program for you involves." We must believe that God is looking out for our best interests. We have to believe that He knows best and that we can relax and accept the way He is leading us.

Probably the most recognized form of discipline the Lord uses with us is *educational discipline*. This is where God teaches us about Himself and moves us along in our trust in Him.

Let's return to the family as an illustration. My mom and dad disciplined me so I would be able to function as a successful adult in society. My parents taught me the discipline of hard work, of finishing a job, of doing my best, of saving money. All of these things were and are important to me. These habits did not form overnight but developed through my childhood and teenage years. Some of these disciplines didn't really take hold until I was an adult, but the training laid the groundwork for success. My parents educated me in how to be a husband, a father, and a provider for my family. They were my most important human teachers regarding life.

God uses educational discipline to teach us about His character and life with Him. Think of what Job learned about God as a result of all he went through. He could not have learned those things about the greatness of God any other way. How many times have we listened to people share about the hard times they've gone through? They often say, "I wouldn't trade that experience for anything in the world, but I wouldn't want to go through that again either!" Both of those statements are true! We wouldn't trade that difficult experience because through it we learned something new about God. He revealed Himself to us, and no one can take that away. Our new knowledge of God is forever etched into our souls. Our faith grows through the storms of life, not on our vacations to Hawaii. And yet, we wouldn't want to go through the trial again because it was painful and uncomfortable. It's right after we have the flu that we appreciate good health the most. The Lord's discipline results in the joy of knowing God for ourselves, and that deepens our faith. The bad makes the good so much better.

Drill sergeants in the Marine Corps are not the most loved people in the world. But Glenn began to understand that even though they were hard, strict, and loud, they knew what was best for the new recruits. Their sole purpose was to teach their squads how to survive in war. Glenn's attitude toward his drill instructor changed when he realized that he was on his side and that he was there to help him succeed and live. That instructor might one day save his life through the discipline and teaching he gave day after day during those four months of torturous training. Glenn had become a Christian, and he now saw God to be like a drill instructor. The instructor asks recruits to do the unknown for the unseen, and those recruits had to trust that there was a purpose to it all.

Does God not do the same with us? Do we trust Him? Do we have faith that He is on our side and has a good purpose for allowing or causing the things we are going through? Are we patient with what God is doing in our lives even when we don't understand?

Our lack of patience tells us what we really believe about God! Why wait for God when we can go ahead and do it ourselves? Why wait when someone else might beat us to the opportunity? Why wait when we know this is what we want to do? Why wait when there seems to be no reason to do so? Are you a microwave or a Crock-Pot? Do you have to have everything *now*? Do you push and claw your way to the forefront of opportunities? Or do you move ahead at God's pace, trusting Him?

I find myself being compelled to read about Joseph over and over again. I think the draw is because in his life I can see the three kinds of disciplines that the Lord uses.

The story begins in Genesis 37. Israel loved his son Joseph more than his other children because he was born to him later in life. In any family, favoritism does not go unnoticed by the other children. And Jacob was blatant about it—he even made Joseph a special robe for all the other children to see. Not smart parenting here. Then Joseph had a wild dream about grain, symbolizing all of his brothers bowing down to him. In Joseph's pride, pride that his father helped foster, he told his brothers about the dream. Not too smart, Joseph. His brothers knew exactly what the dream was about. Someday they would bow before him? How absurd! "Do you intend to reign over us?" they asked Joseph. "Will you actually rule us?" (verse 8). Their dislike of the spoiled child grew into hatred, and they decided it was time to make him disappear.

With all of its twists and turns, Joseph's story is like a modern mystery. The brothers sold their little brother into slavery, concocting a story that he had been eaten by a wild animal. Jacob was devastated by the loss of his favorite son, but all the brothers except Reuben were glad to see him gone. Was this injustice toward Joseph really the will of God? Did God really want Joseph taken from his family and sold into slavery?

Things went from bad to worse for Joseph. He was sold to Potiphar, an Egyptian official. The Bible says that the Lord blessed Joseph even as a slave and that all he did was successful. Joseph seemed to be on the rebound from his brothers' evil deed. Then Potiphar's wife got the hots for this good-looking teenager and tried to entice him to have sex with her. Joseph did the smart thing, the hard thing—he ran away from her. But circumstantial evidence—his torn clothes in her hand—validated her lie that he had tried to attack her. She couldn't handle his rejection, so she thought she'd teach him a lesson. He went to jail for attempted rape.

Even in jail the Lord made Joseph to prosper, so that the warden gave him a great deal of responsibility and freedom. While in prison Joseph discovered a God-given talent to understand and interpret dreams. Word got around and soon he was interpreting the dreams of the Pharaoh of Egypt himself! Joseph told the Pharaoh of an impending famine and how he should prepare for it. Pharaoh was so impressed that he appointed Joseph to an outstanding position of authority. "Then Pharaoh said to Joseph, 'Since God has made all this known to you, there is no one so discerning and wise as you. You shall be in charge of my palace, and all my people are to submit to your orders. Only with respect to the throne will I be greater than you'" (Genesis 41:39-40). Joseph went from prisoner to prince! Maybe God was in this after all.

Later when the famine was in full swing, Joseph's brothers went to Egypt to buy food. Joseph was in charge, and in a strange twist of fate his brothers came and bowed down to him asking for grain. Though they did not recognize Joseph, Joseph recognized them. After months of playing cat and mouse with his brothers, Joseph finally revealed himself to them at a dinner party. One can only imagine the horror the brothers felt as they realized they had been found out, and the very one they'd harmed could now destroy them. As his brothers recoiled in fear, Joseph reassured them, "And now, do not be distressed and do not be angry with yourselves for selling me here, because it was to save lives that God sent me ahead of you. . . . So then, it was not you who sent me here, but God" (Genesis 45:5, 8). After years of slavery, false accusations, and a rise to power, Joseph could clearly look back and see the hand of God in the events of his life. God had him right where He needed him.

Joseph burst into tears when he told his brothers who he was. Imagine the relief that filled his soul as he came to understand why he had suffered so much. Not understanding what God is doing drains our emotions. Some people such as Joseph get their answer to the question "Why?" Others such as Job must be content with the knowledge that it is better to know God than to know all the answers. Both Joseph and Job had a reason to be bitter, humanly speaking; but they believed God had a better vantage point and trusted His goodness and His sovereignty. Joseph said it so well in Genesis 50:20—"You intended to harm me, but God intended it for good to accomplish what is now being done, the saving of many lives."

"But I trust in you, O LORD; I say, 'You are my God.' My times are in your hands" (Psalm 31:14-15). Do we really believe our times are in the hands of the Lord? Or do we feel like we need to push, promote, and power our way forward? Can it be that when we so quickly say the Lord has led us, in reality we have manipulated our circumstances to get us where we are? I have certainly done that at times. I have run ahead of God because I thought I knew better; I thought He needed my help, only to find that I had really made a mess of things.

God may be calling you to wait. As the late pastor Vance Havner said, "Simply wait upon Him. So doing, we shall be directed, supplied, protected, corrected, and rewarded."

God calls you to be patient while He performs His work in you. Our workaholic society sneers at patience, but those of us who have had to wait on God know it can be the most difficult work of all and yet also the most rewarding.

A man came up to me one night after I had preached in his church. He had no idea I was wrestling with God about the direction of my life. He said, "Remember, a soldier never moves until he gets his orders from his commander!" I wish I could tell you I've always listened to the Lord. But I haven't, and I paid a heavy price. I haven't always trusted God, and that error produced impatience that has impacted and hurt my entire family.

How much better it is when we indeed wait on Him, trust Him, and remain faithful to Him.

Chapter 8

TO KNOW HIM IS TO TRUST HIM

A. W. Tozer wrote in *The Knowledge of the Holy,* "Most of us know God by inference." We know about God by what others tell us about Him—our ministers, conference speakers, books. But sometimes we don't know or experience God for ourselves; we only know about Him. Do we really experience God in our lives, or are we just going through the motions, happy to be part of an ecclesiastical club?

I have met scores of people who have said that until they had an encounter with the living Christ, church was just a social club, a place to meet friends or make business contacts, a function to make them feel better about themselves. In his wonderful study called *Experiencing God,* Henry Blackaby wrote that we will never be satisfied just to know about God, that in fact our souls will be restless until we go beyond the natural and experience the supernatural. As a result of the emptiness of "playing church," many Christians have been propelled to "follow hard after God," as one man expressed it. J. B. Phillips put it in a precise way: "The great difference between present-day

Christianity and that of which we read in the New Testament is that to us, it is primarily a performance; to them it was a real experience" (*Peter's Portrait of Jesus*).

When I speak at men's conferences, attendees often tell me that they find it difficult to trust God. I often ask them, "How well do you know Him?" On most occasions the head drops a bit, the eyes fog up, and the confessions begin. I don't ask them this question to make them feel guilty but to reveal that it's hard to trust someone we don't know. We see lots of people every day whom we wouldn't trust with the keys to our home or the safety of our children. Why? Because we don't know them; we only know about them. It's hard to trust God if we don't know Him personally or very well. If that is the case, we are susceptible to many misconceptions about God that will damage or destroy our trust in Him.

In *Your God Is Too Small,* J. B. Phillips writes about such misconceptions. For instance, he describes a "heavenly policeman" who is always out to get us and to keep us from having fun or enjoying life. The "nice old man" up in the sky is another misconception. *God was good enough for Grandma and Grandpa, but He's outdated for me. He surely cannot understand my world and what my life is like.* God is also perceived by some as a "busy telephone operator" who is frantically connecting and disconnecting people. God is too busy to have time for us.

Deb and I have been married for twenty-two years. We were good friends in high school, serious friends as we entered college, and engaged by the end of our third year in college. We were married a month after we both received our college degrees and went directly into the ministry. I think after all of these years it's safe to say that I trust her and she trusts me. How long has it taken to develop that trust? Oh, about twenty-two years! Trust comes a little at a time through the everyday experiences of life. Trust is built through the good times and the difficult times. Trust is built through laughter and intimacy. Trust comes from sitting and talking in the evening or going on a vacation without the kids. It comes from fighting and making up, from quiet companionship in the car, from taking a walk together. Trust grows one shared experience at a time. Trust builds trust. And faith builds faith.

How do I develop trust in God? Yes, I have received His gift of salvation, and I know I have eternal life. But how can I trust Him with my future, my finances, my relationships, and the things that are worrying me right now? We must start with today! Not tomorrow or next week, but today. Most of us are either prisoners of our past, with feelings of guilt and remorse, or are so concerned about the future with all of its uncertainties that we miss today. God is in *today*. God is with you *now*. At this very moment God is working in your life, and that work is motivated by the love He has for you.

Alexander MacLaren, the Scottish scholarly minister of another era, wrote, "No man loveth God, except the man who has first learned that God loves him." How can I trust God today, or any day for that matter, if I do not believe God really loves me? We know that God so loved the world, but we're not so sure He loves us. The head of the psychology department at an evangelical seminary told me that she felt the number one spiritual issue of the students she counsels is that they don't really believe God loves them. To think that we are training and preparing young men and women to share the love of God with the world, and yet many of them question God's love for them. What if Alexander MacLaren is right? What if we cannot love God until we feel that He loves us? What if we cannot trust Him until we believe that He does truly love us, just as a father loves his children? We must be utterly convinced that God loves us.

"God is love," John writes in 1 John 4:16. Are we convinced of that attribute of our Creator? For me, it has taken a reeducation to firmly believe that God is for me and that He really does desire to be an ongoing part of my life. There have been dark days when I believed that God loved the world but was sure He didn't love me. I was convinced that even though He created me, He must not be happy with what He'd made. I was sure that God not only didn't love me, but He didn't really like me either. When you approach life with that misconception of God, it is impossible to have the thoughts of peace and joy that come from trusting in God. If God is out to get you, there isn't much hope for your daily life.

I can remember the season in my life when I began to pray that God would "unteach" me many of the things I had been taught. I had been taught rules and regulations, duty and obedience, sacrifice and surrender, but little of the love and grace of God. I recently read Philip Yancey's book *The Jesus I Never Knew* and realized we'd gone to similar churches having a legalistic approach to life. As I began to pray that God would teach me anew about Himself, it seemed that the Lord started with His attribute of love. An article I read several years ago in *Psychology Today* confirmed what I already felt in my soul. It said, "Given one wish in life, most of us would wish to be loved." God has created us for love. We have the capacity to give love and to receive love. To be loved and accepted is a driving force in our human experience. "What a man desires is unfailing love." Life defends that declaration from the book of Proverbs (19:22). Men and women need to be loved and appreciated. We want to know that we fill a special place in someone's life. We desire "unfailing love."

Several years ago God began to use my family and family experiences to teach me three important aspects of God's love for me. I'm still learning these lessons, and I at times still struggle with faulty thinking about God. I can, however, stop when dark clouds of doubt linger overhead and say three things that

I know are true about God's love: God's love is uninfluenced; God's love is unending; and God's love is unselfish.

GOD'S LOVE IS *UNINFLUENCED*

Manipulation rules our society at every level—by the media, advertisers, people—and we return it. As children we are taught that if we do something good, someone might like us more. If I do something nice for someone, maybe he'll do something nice for me. As we get older, we raise the stakes in romantic relationships and elsewhere. If I do this for you, maybe you'll like me more. If I buy you something you like, maybe you'll do something for me. Most of us have had the experience of trying to earn someone's approval. We have tried to make someone love us more. Sometimes it works, and sometimes it doesn't.

Thankfully God is not like us. We cannot manipulate God in any way. You and I cannot make God love us more, and we cannot make God love us less. Let me repeat that, because it took me years to understand this. *We cannot make God love us more, and we cannot make God love us less!*

Do you believe that? You cannot make God love you more by doing something for Him. He will not love you more because of some sacrifice you make for His sake. I remember when it finally became clear to me that I couldn't influence God to love me more, because up until then I thought I had to earn the love of God. I used to think, *God, You are going to really love me today because I'm going to have my devotions, and I'm going to spend time praying for missionaries, and, God, You are going to really love me more because I am going to give to the church.* I was forever working at influencing God to love me more. What an incredible relief to finally understand that I have all of God's love that there is. I am His child, and He loves me—that's all there is to it. My children don't have to earn my love; they have it every moment because they are part of me. And the same is true for God and His children.

I couldn't influence God to love me more, and just as thrilling was the understanding that I couldn't make God love me any less. I might wake up in the morning and think, *O God, You're not going to love me as much today as You did yesterday. God, I got mad at my wife and said some unkind things, so I know You don't love me like You did previously. Lord, I had some lustful thoughts, so I know You don't love me like You once did.* Not so! Can I miss out on some of the blessings God has for me because of my sin? Yes. But will God ever stop loving me? No. God doesn't fluctuate in His emotions like we do. We love one day and not the next. There's nothing that I can do as a child of God to make God love me more or less. Our human love is based so much on appearance, performance, and status. We love because of how someone looks or how well they do something to impress us or because of their status and position in life. Praise the Lord that His love is not based on those things at all. "May the glory of the LORD endure forever; may the LORD rejoice in his works" (Psalm 104:31). That includes us! You and I are some of the "works" of the Lord that He rejoices in and loves.

When I first began to travel internationally, I was often away from home for up to three weeks at a time. This was always hard for me physically and emotionally. Physically because I have a bad back that can give me major trouble, especially in stressful situations. Emotionally it was even more difficult having to be gone from Deb and my sons, who were just little guys at the time. As they would drop me off at the airport, I would say good-bye to each of them in a special way. For a long time I saved the oldest son for last because of his emotional response. As a five-year-old he would always say, "Dad, you're going to come back, aren't you?" It was half question, half statement. How do you think I responded? Did I put my hands on my hips and with no expression or emotion at all say, "Ben, I'll miss you. Be good, and I'll see you in three weeks. Goodbye"? Is that how I reassured my son? Of course not. When Ben would ask if I was coming back, I'd get down on my knees, grab his little face, and make sure he was looking at me. Then with all the emotion of a father who loves his son, I'd say, "Ben, you are the greatest little boy in the world. I miss you so much when I'm gone that sometimes I even cry. I take your picture with me wherever I go. I love you, and of course I'm coming back. I'll bring you a surprise when I return."

Sometimes I think the Lord tires of the emotionless way in which we read the Scriptures. When we read, "Never will I leave you; never will I forsake you" (Hebrews 13:5), do we read with emotion, or do we read in the monotone voice of a robot? I think the Lord wants us to read it with all the emotion of a loving father toward his child. "NEVER will I leave you!" God has created the love and passion that fathers and mothers have for their children. God has those same emotions for us, but in a completely pure and holy way. God's love for us is neither influenced by our spiritually beneficial activities nor by our spiritual detours. The story of the prodigal son is such an awesome reminder of the father-heart of God who keeps watching for our return. We've all been prodigal sons and daughters and have known the joy of returning to our Father to be forgiven and restored. We cannot make God love us more, and we cannot make Him love us less. Believe it!

GOD'S LOVE IS ALSO *UNENDING*

God's love never stops or ceases, which is quite significant in a society that nearly boasts of infidelity and betrayal. Most of us are connected in some way with individuals who said they would love forever but didn't. Despite the devastating consequences, divorce in America is an accepted norm. Can we really find a love that is unending? Yes! God proclaims, "I have loved you with an everlasting love; I have drawn you with loving-kindness" (Jeremiah 31:3). God's love for us is unending; it never ends.

My first girlfriend in high school used to write passionate letters that she would always end with, "Love you forever." But she didn't love me forever. In fact, she dumped me after eight months for a better-looking guy and broke my heart. People promise to love us forever, but only God stays perfectly true to His promise.

We can be encouraged by Romans 8:35: "Who shall separate us from the love of Christ? Shall trouble or hardship or persecution or famine or nakedness or danger or sword?" When the apostle Paul wrote these inspired words, he had gone through all of these things except the sword. Paul was saying that when we go through difficult times we sense the love of God in an even greater measure. The pain of life requires the medicine of God's love. When the chaplain of the Portland Trailblazers first shared with me that he had lost his teenage daughter in a car accident, he smiled when he said it was during that awful time of grief that he felt the love and nearness of God more than at any other time in his life. When we go through hard times, and we all do, we can experience the Father's love for us as He sustains us and gives us comfort.

Many years ago Ben was running around in our backyard when he tripped and fell face first into the side of our deck. I heard the awful thud and knew he was badly hurt. As I ran over to him to pick him up, he lifted his face off the ground, and there was blood everywhere. I'm not sure which was worse, his screaming or the blood. My heart was pounding as I scooped him into my arms and headed for the house. Deb came running only to find her little boy with blood pouring out of his mouth. She was tending to Jordan at the time, so she couldn't grab him out of my arms, which just about killed her. You know how mothers are when their kids get hurt. I told her not to worry and that I could take care of the situation, though I'm sure she had her doubts.

When Ben had collided with the deck, he'd jammed his teeth into his gums. Once the bleeding subsided and our doctor and dentist both told us he probably didn't need medical attention, I sat down with Ben in my reclining chair. Back we went, Ben on my lap with one of my arms around him and the other holding ice inside his upper lip. His crying quieted, and my parental fears diminished. After about thirty minutes, I asked Ben if he wanted to get down from my lap, and he assured me he did not! Forty-five minutes passed, and I asked Ben if he wanted to get down and play with his toys. No, he didn't. I checked again after an hour, and he assured me that he was quite comfortable where he was. Finally after about an hour and twenty minutes, Ben decided he could get down and play again.

Up until that day, the longest I'd ever held Ben on my lap was about fifteen minutes, but that day, the day before Easter, I held him for an hour and twenty minutes! Why? First, Ben knew he was hurt. Second, he knew I wouldn't make him get down. And third, with my arms wrapped around him as I kissed him on the head, Ben knew I loved him. He felt the pain that came from his fall, but he also felt the unending love that came from his father.

We all experience pain in many forms. No matter what kind of hurt we are experiencing, we have the blessing of being able to go to our Father. There have been times when I could almost feel the arms of God holding me as I sat on His lap. I could almost hear the comforting voice of the Father say, "Well, Dan, do you want to get down now?" And I responded, "Not yet, Lord. I still hurt." "Dan, it's been a month now—do you want Me to let you go?" "No, Lord, just keep holding on."

It seems like only such hurts bring a greater understanding and appreciation of God our Father.

We have no idea how attractive to God we are. From the earliest years of my Christian life, it was drilled into my head that God loves the sinner but hates the sin. That sounded good, but the way it was presented, I never really came away feeling encouraged. I felt more like God hates the sin and the sinner as a result of the sin. Living in Oregon for so many years, we had to battle the rain and the ensuing mud that our boys always seemed to find. When they would come through the back door with mud on their feet, I would send them back out. Was I rejecting my sons? Did I do something that showed I didn't care about them? No! I rejected the mud on their shoes that would dirty the carpet, which would cost me money to clean. I sent them back out and told them to clean the mud off their shoes and then they could come back in. I wanted them in the warm house and out of the cold and rain, but without the mud. God rejects our sin, but He doesn't reject us! In fact, He offers to cleanse us from sin as we confess it to Him. God is for us, He loves us, and He does like us.

I have three sons and no daughters, which means I may not have to spend as much money when my children get married. Though I might be better off financially, I have lost out on that wonderful relationship between a dad and his daughter. Through the years as I've watched my father-in-law deal with his daughter, my wife, I've learned that it is a very special relationship. Years ago I took the "chicken" way out and wrote a letter to Deb's dad, asking him if I could marry his daughter. I was in college at the time. To my surprise, he called me and began to ask several questions about love, commitment, finances, employment, and my future. You see, he had raised Deb from a baby, investing time and money in his most prized possession. He was there when she got hurt as a little girl. He was there in the hospital when she had surgery as a teenager. He paid for the braces on her teeth. He had saved for years and was now investing his money in her education. What my father-in-law wanted to know was, "Will you take care of her as well as I have? Will you love her as I have?" I promised that I would, and a year later we were married.

Twenty-two years of marriage have passed, and many changes have occurred in our lives. But there has been one constant in all this time—a weekly telephone call from Deb's dad. Yes, every weekend for twenty-two years he has called on Saturday morning to check in with his daughter and the rest of the family. Bob was a concerned father, and he still is. As James Dobson says, "Once you have children you worry about them forever!"

What a wonderful picture of the love of God. God is a concerned, doting father who is interested in every area of our lives. The psalmist prayed, "Keep me as the apple of your eye" (Psalm 17:8)—another way of saying, "Keep me in the center of Your eye," the most tender portion, the most sensitive, protected by the eye socket and the eyelid. We are the center of God's attention and affection. Have you ever thought about how much God loves you?

GOD'S LOVE IS *UNSELFISH*

We like to think of God's love in terms of His granting our requests, though He also says no when He knows that what we're asking for would be bad for us. But God is indeed generous, and He provides good gifts. When we love, we give to the one we feel affection for. Amy Carmichael wrote, "You can give without loving, but you cannot love without giving." When I knew I wanted to marry Deb, I knew I not only would have to get her father's permission but also would have to buy an engagement ring. I had only one possession that was of any value—my motorcycle. I had saved long and hard for that bike, and I was especially attached to it because it was my first one. But I loved Deb, and I wanted to marry her; so I sold my bike for just enough money to buy a ring. I loved, so I gave! After we were married I bought another bike; so I got the girl and the bike. What a deal!

God gives us many things, but none is greater than His attention. God has time for you and me. God is not so busy that He puts us off until another day. When we come to God, we don't have to go through a menu and answer a lot of questions. Because of the substitutionary death of Jesus Christ, we can go directly to God, and He listens. Psalm 139 teaches us that we are never out of His sight or His care.

When I came to Christ as a teenager, I was taught to memorize Scripture. It was one of those duties of being a "good Christian." Because I have a lazy streak, I decided to memorize the shortest verses I could find. One of them was 1 Peter 5:7, "Casting all your care upon him; for he careth for you." *King James Version*, of course. Those words really didn't mean much to me at the time, though in subsequent years I would lean heavily upon them. Later on, going through some rough waters, I recalled those words and decided to look up the verse in other translations and paraphrases. In *The Living Bible* I read, "Let him have all your worries and cares, for he is always thinking about you and watching everything that concerns you." And the *Phillips* paraphrase says, "You can throw the whole weight of your anxieties upon him, for you are his personal concern." Let those words sink deep into your soul. God says He is "always thinking about you" and that "you are his personal concern"! I don't always think about my wife, and my wife doesn't always think about me, but God is always thinking about us.

How can God be thinking of me and be thinking of all the other Christians who live on this earth? How can I be His personal concern along with all the Christians in Africa, Asia, Europe, and the entire world? While sitting in a doctor's office, I picked up a magazine and read a fascinating article on things in our universe that move incredibly fast. The example that caught my imagination was the quartz crystal that many of us have in our watches. We know that everything in our universe is made of atoms and molecules. Scientists have discovered that the molecular structure of the quartz crystal vibrates nine billion times in one second. Nine billion vibrations in one second! As I read that fact, I thought, *If God can think that fast, which He can since He created something that moves like that, then I can believe He's always thinking about me.* God is always thinking about you because you are His personal concern.

Today you might feel abandoned and alone. You might think that God isn't really that interested in you. Do yourself and God a favor and ask Him to reveal Himself to you as He really is—a loving Father. Ask God to identify and change the misconceptions you have had about Him. Ask God to heal you of your negative thinking about His opinion of you. If you have personally invited Jesus Christ to be your Savior and Lord, to forgive you for your sins and make you brand-new from the inside out, you are a child of God, and God loves His children. How can you trust God every day if every day you wake up with the thought that God is mad at you? How can you experience the joy of the Lord when you entertain the thought that God must be disappointed in you? How can you look at your situation with the confidence that God is with you when you are poisoned by doubts that God is at all interested in you? Remember, "You can throw the whole weight of your anxieties upon him, for you are his personal concern!"

A CLOSING STORY

Few things in life are as fulfilling as a family vacation—that wonderful time when everyone in the family can just be themselves and enjoy the company of those they love the most.

With all of the international travel that I do, it doesn't take me long to acquire a great number of frequent-flier miles. So one summer I decided to take the family on the ultimate vacation—Hawaii! I cashed in a ton of miles, flew my wife and two sons to Maui first-class, and put us all up at the Westin Maui. If there was ever going to be a perfect vacation, this was going to be it. The Westin is an incredible resort with five pools connected by waterslides, and the beach is only a stone's throw away. What a place for the kids!

One night Deb and I sat on the edge of our bed looking into the faces of our two sons as they lay fast asleep on their bed. Their skin had become a little browner from all the time they were spending in the pool and the waves. As I looked at their faces, it seemed as if they were actually smiling in their sleep. They were content with their lives as they were, and even more content with the vacation that Dad had provided for them.

As Deb and I sat there in a rare moment of relaxation and stillness, I began to think about the reaction of my sons to this "perfect" vacation. I realized that not once had my sons ever asked me, "Dad, are you sure you have enough money for the plane tickets?" I didn't tell them they were free; why not let them think I'm richer than I am? They never asked me, "Hey, Dad, are you sure you have enough money for this great hotel?" They never worried if I had enough money for the meals we ate or for the souvenirs I bought them. They never asked about the resources I had for this vacation. They just kept on asking for things, like, "Dad, can we go to the Hard Rock Café for lunch?"

It dawned on me at that moment that they did not have a care in the world! They trusted me, and they knew I was going to take care of them on this trip. They knew from past experience that Dad might be a little tight with money during the year, but when vacation time comes, the money flows. They knew that Dad would never take them on a trip like this without planning it all out and making sure there was enough of everything for every situation. (Yes, I still have a little "control freak" left in me!) They trusted Dad.

As I looked at their little faces, so happy and content, I thought to myself, *I would love to be a child like that again!* No worries, no cares, no fears! It was then that the Holy Spirit of God spoke to me in a fresh way. *Dan, you can still be a child like that if you will only trust Me like your children trust you.* I am sure the Lord did not mean that my life would be simple and carefree like my sons were experiencing at that time. But God did invite me to be a child once again. I have found that it is okay to be a child again and to live in childlike faith in Elohim. In fact, it is God's desire for us to continue to live as His children. He even told the disciples, who were adults, "I tell you the truth, unless you change and become like little children, you will never enter the kingdom of heaven" (Matthew 18:3).

True joy and contentment are not found in the absence of problems or pain, but in the ever-abiding presence of our loving heavenly Father. Today your Father cries out to you with outstretched arms, "Trust Me!" "Trust Me first, not last." "Trust Me because there is nobody else in all of the universe who loves you like I do!"

We can trust Him, not as a last resort, but day in and day out, moment by moment, knowing He cares for us!

A Word About the Author and Eternity Minded Ministries

Over the past twenty years across America and in thirty-seven countries, Dan Owens has proclaimed the Gospel of Jesus Christ and has communicated the need for personal renewal to hundreds of thousands of people.

Christianity Today recently profiled Dan Owens as one of fifty "Up and Comers"—one of "the many faithful disciples God has raised up to lead the church into the new millennium." This recognition came because of his unique ability to adapt his contemporary messages to impact any audience. The British publication *Evangelism Today* says, "Dan Owens has a winsome way with words, making it possible to say anything without giving offense."

Dan is also the author of *Sharing Christ When You Feel You Can't* (Crossway) and has helped train thousands of Christians to build bridges to their unchurched world with his "Building Bridges for Eternity" seminar.

Before he founded Eternity Minded Ministries, Dan served with the Luis Palau Evangelistic Association as Director of Training and an Associate Evangelist for eleven years. He lives with his wife and three children in San Diego, California.

Dan is a graduate of Christian Heritage College (San Diego, California) and Multnomah Seminary (Portland, Oregon). An approved Staley lecturer for colleges and universities, Dan has been a featured speaker at youth events across the country and around the world.

Whether speaking to thousands of teenagers at a rally, college students at a university, adults at a missions conference, or families at a festival, Dan is at home in front of people. Listening to this fun, dynamic, and compelling speaker, audiences are moved to consider *eternity*!

For more information contact:

ETERNITY MINDED MINISTRIES

P.O. Box 502101

San Diego, California 92150

Voice: 858-675-9477

Mobile: 619-807-8581

Fax: 858-673-8603

E-mail: OwensEMM@aol.com